C000151655

Joseph Bettey was formerly Reader in Local History at the University of Bristol. He has been interested in the history of Dorset for many years, and has contributed numerous articles to the *Proceedings* of Dorset Natural History and Archaeological Society, and to other publications. His research has included work on records relating to historic agriculture, rural society and church life in the county, and among his numerous books are: *Dorset* (1974), *Rural Life in Wessex* (1977 & 1987), *The Landscape of Wessex* (1980), *Wessex from AD 1000* (1986), *Church and Parish* (1987), *Suppression of the Monasteries in the West Country* (1989), *Estates and the English Countryside* (1993), *Man and the Land* (with Jo Draper) (1996), and 'Discover Dorset' *Farming* (2000). His most recent book is *Wiltshire Farming in the Seventeenth Century* (2005).

*Following page*
The gabled bay on the east front of Waterston House is dated 1586, two years before the defeat of the Spanish Armada, and is a superb testament to the inventiveness and self-confidence of the Elizabethan Age. When built, probably by Thomas Howard, a son of Lord Howard of Bindon, it was the height of new architectural fashion, as represented by the three Classical orders: Doric columns either side of the entrance, Ionic on the second stage and as mullions in the three-light window, and Corinthian columns at the top. The two lower figures are holding palm branches, whilst below the gable and the pair of rampant lions on either side of the circular window stands the figure of Justice with her scales.

## DISCOVER DORSET

# TUDORS & STUARTS

J.H. BETTEY

THE DOVECOTE PRESS

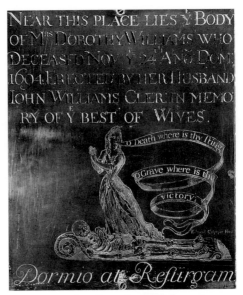

Memorial to Dorothy Williams, 1694,
Pimperne church.

First published in 2006 by The Dovecote Press Ltd
Stanbridge, Wimborne Minster, Dorset BH21 4JD

ISBN 1 904349 40 4

© J.H. Bettey 2006

J.H. Bettey has asserted his rights under the Copyright, Designs
and Patent Act 1988 to be identified as author of this work

Typeset in Monotype Sabon
Printed and bound by Baskerville Press, Salisbury, Wiltshire

All papers used by The Dovecote Press are natural, recyclable products made
from wood grown in sustainable, well-managed forests

A CIP catalogue record for this book is available
from the British Library

*All rights reserved*

1 3 5 7 9 8 6 4 2

# CONTENTS

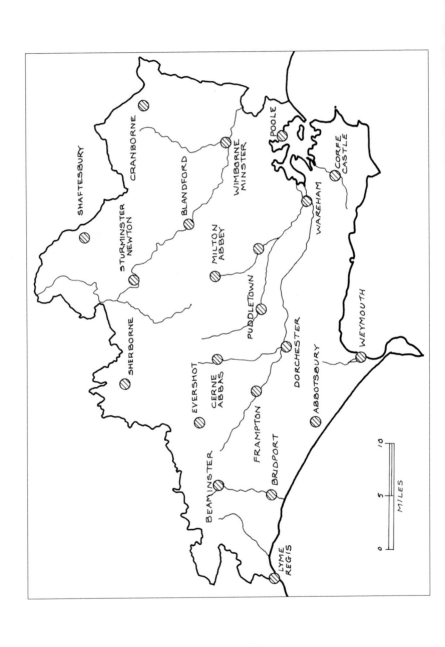

SHAFTESBURY

CRANBORNE

STURMINSTER
NEWTON

BLANDFORD

WIMBORNE
MINSTER

POOLE

CORFE
CASTLE

MILTON
ABBEY

WAREHAM

PUDDLETOWN

SHERBORNE

EVERSHOT

CERNE
ABBAS

DORCHESTER

WEYMOUTH

FRAMPTON

ABBOTSBURY

BEAMINSTER

BRIDPORT

LYME
REGIS

0        5        10

MILES

# SETTING THE SCENE

When King Richard III was killed at the battle of Bosworth in 1485, and Henry Tudor seized the Crown, inaugurating the Tudor dynasty, this dramatic national event had little immediate impact on most of the people living in Dorset.

In 1485 Dorset was a predominantly agricultural county with a population of some 60,000 people, most of them living in small rural communities or isolated farms. Towns such as Dorchester, Shaftesbury, Sherborne, Wimborne and Blandford were important as markets, but few of them had more than 1000 inhabitants. Ships leaving Dorset ports with cloth returned laden with wine, fruit, dye-stuffs, spices and olive oil. The antiquarian, John Leland, who visited

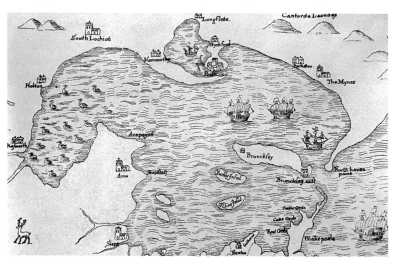

*Above* Plan of Poole Harbour in 1585 by the Elizabethan cartographer, Ralph Treswell. 'The Mynes' shown near the church at Parkstone were producing alum and copperas.

*Opposite page* Dorset in 1600, showing the market towns.

An early-seventeenth century view of Poole showing the crowded shipping in the harbour, the surrounding heathland, and the windmill on Baiter which was first erected in 1542.

Dorset in 1542, noted the trade between Lyme Regis and France. Also sharing in overseas trade were the ports of Weymouth and Melcombe Regis, which after centuries of squabbling were forcibly united by royal charter in 1571. Leland commented on the busy port of Poole, the 'fair buildings' in the town, and the great increase in its trade 'within living memory by reason of merchandise'. Later Poole was to become even more prosperous through its involvement in the lucrative Newfoundland fishing trade. Its importance was recognised in 1568 when it was granted a royal charter giving it the status of a county.

The later fifteenth century had seen increasing prosperity in the county, largely due to the wealth created by wool and the production of woollen cloth. The principal markets were at Dorchester, Sherborne and Shaftesbury, and there were several smaller markets, such as Beaminster, Frampton, Evershot, Cerne Abbas, Stalbridge, Sturminster Newton, Bere Regis and Cranborne, where only the traces of the former market places survive as reminders of their past importance. Even more significant were the annual fairs, both for commerce and for social life. The greatest of the Dorset fairs was held in September each year on a bare hill-top at Woodbury Hill near Bere Regis. The fair attracted buyers and sellers from all over southern England, and vast numbers of sheep and cattle changed hands, as well as cheese, butter, cloth, canvass, leather goods, knives, tools and trinkets. Today nothing on the hill indicates the former importance of this fair.

What does survive, however, is evidence of the wealth derived from the trade in wool and cloth that can be seen in the late-medieval work

One of the wooden figures from the fine nave roof of Bere Regis church. The roof was paid for by Cardinal John Morton (d.1500), who was born nearby at Milborne St Andrew.

in so many Dorset churches. The splendid architecture of churches such as Beaminster, Yetminster, Cerne Abbas, Bradford Abbas, Bere Regis and many others is impressive testimony to the prosperity and piety of those parishioners who financed the expensive work. One notable benefactor to the church at Bere Regis was Cardinal John Morton, who was born nearby at Milborne St Andrew. He was educated first at Cerne Abbey and later at Oxford, and rose rapidly through the Church and by service to Henry VII. It was Morton who stabilised the royal finances and ensured Henry's continuing grasp of the throne. He combined the offices of Lord Chancellor and Archbishop of Canterbury, and in 1493 he was created a Cardinal. Having acquired great wealth, he founded a chantry chapel in Bere Regis church where his mother's family, the Turbervilles, were buried, and he also helped to pay for the finest and most elaborately-carved timber roof in Dorset, decorated with painted figures representing the twelve apostles.

The Strangways' mansion at Melbury Samford. The central part, with the prospect tower, was built by Giles Strangways in about 1530. The house was greatly enlarged by later members of the family.

Likewise, the fine late-medieval and early Tudor manor houses such as Athelhampton, Purse Caundle, Parnham, and Wolfeton illustrate the wealth of Dorset's landowners. One of the largest houses was built at Melbury Samford by Sir Giles Strangways, whose wealth came from shrewd estate management and large-scale sheep rearing. Later he became even more wealthy through his service to Henry VIII over the dissolution of the Dorset monasteries. The fortune acquired through trade and commerce by Sir William Martyn, who was lord mayor of London in 1493, enabled him to build the house at Athelhampton, as well as to endow a private chapel in the parish church at Puddletown, now full of family monuments displaying the Martyn emblem of an ape and mirror with the sinister slogan 'Whoso looks at Martyn's ape, Martyn's ape shall look at him'.

The alabaster effigy of Sir William Martyn of Athelhampton in Puddletown church, with the Martyn emblem of a chained ape at his feet.

It was the profit to be made from wool, together with the use of the sheep-fold for fertilizing the arable land, which led to the creation of the huge sheep flocks which so impressed visitors to Dorset. Leland wrote that there were 'al about great flokkes of sheepe', and the local writer Thomas Gerard in about 1630 described the chalk downland as 'all overspread with innumerable Flockes of Sheepe, from which the Countrie hath reapted an unknownen Gaine'. The importance of sheep and wool in the economy of Dorset was such that when in 1535 Henry VIII ordered an enquiry into the wealth of all of the monasteries in England, the so-called *Valor Ecclesiasticus*, it was only in Dorset, alone among the counties, that sheep numbers were listed as part of monastic wealth. Between them, the seven major monasteries of Dorset possessed no less than 25,093 sheep. Milton Abbey had 1,775 at Milton and a further 5,554 sheep on outlying manors, whilst the nuns at Shaftesbury had 2,300 sheep on their Dorset estates. Similar large flocks were maintained by lay landowners in Dorset.

The profitability of sheep farming brought problems in its train, leading to the decline of arable, the desertion of villages and the eviction of tenants as landowners sought large areas of unimpeded grazing land. During the early sixteenth century the tenants of Sir William Fyllol at Bincombe, near Weymouth, complained of being evicted from their tenements to make room for sheep, while his tenants at nearby Winterborne Came reported that their lands were over-run by sheep, and that they would soon be forced to abandon their homes 'by cause of the saide great opressions'. It is clear that their complaints were in vain, for all along the Winterborne valley, south of Dorchester, there is a string of deserted village sites; Winterborne Herringston, Farringdon, Germayne, Came and Whitcombe. At Winterborne Farringdon only a ruined fragment of the church survives to show the site of the former village (*see page 12*). It was of this village that Thomas Gerard commented in about 1630: '. . . there is hardlie any house left in the Parish, such of late hath beene the Covetousness of some private Men, that to increase their Demesnes have depopulated whole parishes'.

It was the depopulation caused by ever increasing pressure for grazing land for sheep that Shakespeare refers to in *Pericles of Athens* where he compares greedy landowners to whales 'who never leave

The ruins of St German's church on the site of the former village of Winterborne Farringdon, one of a string of deserted villages along the valley south of Dorchester.

gaping till they've swallowed the whole parish, church, steeple, bells and all'. In Dorset, Shakespeare's contemporary poet, Thomas Bastard, vicar of Bere Regis, wrote

'Sheepe have eate up our medows and our downes
Our corne, our wood, whole villages and townes'.

Apart from farming and the cloth trade, there were few other sources of employment for Dorset men and women. Stone was quarried at Purbeck, and there were quarries on Portland, but the great demand for Portland stone only began in the later seventeenth century. The rope, net and sailcloth industry were centred on Bridport, in an area where the rich soils of west Dorset were particularly suited to the cultivation of hemp and flax; and the gloving industry centred on Yeovil provided out-work in north Dorset.

Some coastal settlements had suffered badly from French raids during the fifteenth century and only recovered under the Tudors. Poole, Lyme Regis and Melcombe Regis were attacked on several occasions. Bexington, behind the Chesil Beach west of Abbotsbury, was burnt by the French in 1440, and the inhabitants were either killed or carried off as prisoners. The village never recovered and in 1451 the benefice was united with Puncknowle, 'because of the poverty caused by the attacks of the enemy'. The low value placed on Abbotsbury

Abbey's manor of Portesham was explained by the fact that 'few tenants dare dwell there for fear of the enemies . . . frequently arriving and coming by sea there'.

It was to counter such attacks that a chain of castles and forts were constructed all along the south coast of England during Henry VIII's reign. Four of these were in Dorset. A castle on Brownsea Island to defend the entrance to Poole Harbour (*shown on Treswell's plan of the Harbour on page 7*), a fort at Abbotsbury and castles or fortified gun platforms at Sandsfoot and Portland commanding the entrance to the Harbour. Portland Castle, built of local stone, has survived almost intact, and is an excellent example of the military architecture of the time. It was built during the 1530s and the royal accounts show that it cost £4,964 19s 10¼d. From its low solid outer walls cannon could repulse any enemy attack on shipping within the harbour. Behind the gun emplacements are quarters for the garrison and a magazine for powder and shot. An inscription within the castle reads:

'God save King Henrie the VIII of that name, and Prins Edward, begotten of Quene Jane, my Ladi Mari that goodlie virgin, and the Ladi Elizabeth so towardli, with the Kinges honorable counselers'.

Portland Castle was built in about 1539-40 as part of Henry VIII's scheme of coastal defence. This is one of a series of views of Portland made by the local artist, J.W. Upham, in about 1805.

Eight Dorset towns were Parliamentary boroughs, each returning two members to Parliament. These were Dorchester, Bridport, Shaftesbury, Wareham, Lyme Regis, Poole, Weymouth and Melcombe Regis. The last two continued to have two members of Parliament each, even after they were united in 1571. During the later sixteenth century these eight boroughs were joined by Corfe Castle. Thus the county had eighteen MPs, in addition to the two members representing the county, right up to the Reform Act of 1832.

Most people lived in small, self-contained communities as tenants of one of the great estates that dominated Dorset. As well as those belonging to a handful of major landowners, these included the estates of the Crown, the Duchy of Cornwall, the great monastic houses, and institutions such as King's College, Cambridge, and the colleges of Eton and Winchester. The lives of their tenants were regulated by manorial customs, and enforced by manorial courts that regulated land tenure, farming in the open fields, livestock numbers, property maintenance and petty disputes.

The manor of Piddlehinton provides a good example of a small, rural community. The manor belonged to Eton College and the arable land was in three large open fields, each divided into strips. There was also meadow and pasture land, and extensive grazing on the downland. The lands were divided between the tenant of the college's demesne land, which amounted to 136 acres of arable, the rector, who had forty acres of arable, and the copyhold tenants, 20 having 24 acres of arable and 10 with 12 acres of arable each. All these tenants also had grazing rights for their sheep and cattle on the downland, and the right to a portion of the meadow land for hay. There were in addition 16 cottagers who had only a house and garden, and a water mill at which all tenants were obliged to have their corn ground. The miller was entitled to a 1/24th of all the corn he ground. By the sixteenth century most of the labour services had been commuted for a money payment, but the tenants at Piddlehinton were still obliged to work on the demesne lands at haymaking and during the harvest. A somewhat muddier annual duty took place on the Thursday in Whitsun week, when they were required to clean and scour the mill pond.

# THE REFORMATION

Throughout Dorset during the early Tudor period the wealth, power and influence of the Church were evident everywhere. Few places were more than a couple of miles from a parish church, and the monastic houses, friaries, churches and chapelries were by far the largest and most impressive buildings in the landscape. For successive generations the Church with its festivals, saints' days, processions, rituals, drama and imagery, provided a pattern for the progress of each year and brought colour, music, light, hope and holiday to every community. The remit of the Church courts included matters as various as wills, marriage, slander, immoral behaviour, heresy, and failure to pay tithes or other dues. Common belief and shared concern for the Church buildings, their enlargement, decoration and adornment, provided a focus for community life and an object for fund-raising, merry-making and recreation, while the regular round of services brought the people of each parish together.

The profusion of lights, altars, screens and statues within the parish churches is clear from the surviving examples, and also from occasional documentary evidence. For example, an inventory of All Hallows' church, Sherborne, dated 1508, lists a remarkable array of crosses, candlesticks, silver plate, statues of saints, precious jewels, rosaries, beads, rings and other valuable items which had been acquired over the years. An indication of the brightly-coloured wall paintings with which churches were decorated can be seen in the now-faded examples at Whitcombe, Cerne Abbas, Gussage St Andrew and Tarrant Crawford (*see page 24*).

Dorset was notable for the wealth and splendour of its ancient Benedictine abbeys at Abbotsbury, Cerne, Milton and Sherborne, the wealthy Benedictine nunnery at Shaftesbury, the Cistercian houses at Bindon and Forde, and the Cistercian nunnery at Tarrant, as well as several other foundations, such as the college of priests at Wimborne

Minster, the collegiate foundation at Bridport, the small monastic house at Cranborne which was a dependency of Tewkesbury Abbey in Gloucestershire, and the Augustinian house at Christchurch (then in Hampshire). There were monastic schools at Sherborne, Cerne, Milton and Wimborne, and numerous hospitals or almshouses and charities.

In the decades before the Reformation there is little evidence of any hostility to the Church or disagreement with its doctrines. The reign of Henry VII (1485-1509) and the first part of the reign of his son, Henry VIII, were years of peace and prosperity. Even as late as 1530 few would have foreseen the speed and scope of the changes which the next few years would bring. No-one would have predicted that within ten years there would be no more monks, nuns or friars, and that within twenty years the ancient Latin Mass and Catholic ritual would

The interior of the great hall built at Milton Abbas by Abbot Middleton (1481-1525). It became part of the mansion created by Sir John Tregonwell after the suppression of the abbey.

The elegant abbot's lodging and tower at Forde Abbey, built by the last abbot, Thomas Chard (abbot 1521-39). The high-quality work, fine tower and elaborate carving show the wealth of the abbey and optimism for its future. Following the dissolution in 1539 the church was demolished and the abbey buildings converted into a mansion.

be illegal, shrines, statues, images, paintings and stained glass would be destroyed and that the Bible and services would be in English. The spectacular late-medieval work at Sherborne, the gatehouse which survives at Cerne, Abbot William Middleton's fine hall at Milton, the reredos to the high altar at Christchurch, and Abbot Thomas Chard's palatial lodging and porch at Forde, all suggest that the builders had no inkling that they were soon to be suppressed.

In Dorset and throughout the kingdom, the process of suppression started with the summoning of Parliament in 1529, and the gradual attack on the Pope's power in England, culminating in 1534 with the Act of Supremacy which declared that Henry VIII, not the Pope, was supreme head of the Church of England. Armed with this new power over the Church, and conscious of the Crown's pressing need for money, the King's chief minister, Thomas Cromwell, ordered two major enquiries into the affairs of the monasteries. The first thoroughly investigated all their wealth and income, and in 1535 produced its results in what became known as the *Valor Ecclesiasticus*. This was an enormous undertaking and demonstrated for the first time just how extremely wealthy the monasteries were. It revealed, for example, that Shaftesbury, with its widespread estates, was the richest nunnery in England, with an annual income of £1166 to support its 57 nuns; Sherborne enjoyed £682 per annum for 15 monks, Milton had £578 per annum for 13 monks and Cerne £575 for 17 monks.

The purpose of the second, parallel enquiry was to investigate the state of religious life in the monasteries. The commissioners found few scandals on which they could report to Cromwell concerning the Dorset houses, although the report on Shaftesbury did reveal that one of the nuns, Dorothy Clausey, was an illegitimate daughter of Cardinal Wolsey. Cromwell was, however, provided with the sort of material he needed from Dorset by two apparently disgruntled monks. The first was William Christchurch, a monk of Cerne, who sent a long list of complaints to Cromwell concerning the abbot, Thomas Corton. The abbot was accused of ill-rule, wasting the goods of the monastery and, above all, of inordinate sexual appetite, ignoring his vow of chastity, keeping concubines, having illegitimate children, and 'he openly solicits honest women in the town to have his will of them . . . the farms belongynge to the monastery be in ruyne and decay by the abbot's wilfulness'. Significantly the monk also complained that the abbot had several times disciplined him and that 'he was very ill-handled'. Cromwell also received a letter from William Grey, a monk of Abbotsbury, complaining about the abbot and alleging that he had sold jewels, plate and treasures belonging to the monastery, and also kept women 'not one, two or three, but many'.

Using the material collected by his commissioners and supplied by disaffected monks, Cromwell presented a bill to Parliament suppressing all religious houses with an income of less than £200 per annum. This was passed by Parliament and received the royal assent in March 1536, and all the buildings, estates and property passed to the Crown, while the monks and nuns were sent to the larger houses. In Dorset, only Bindon with an annual income of £147 per annum came within the terms of the Act, but it was allowed to continue after a bribe of £300 to Cromwell.

Next Cromwell turned his attention to the friars. There was a Franciscan friary at Dorchester with seven friars, and a much smaller Dominican friary at Melcombe Regis. Following sustained pressure from Cromwell and his commissioners throughout 1537-8, all the West Country friars were 'persuaded' to surrender their friaries to the Crown. At Dorchester the friars were only induced to surrender with great difficulty. Their long-serving warden, Dr William Germen was held in high esteem in the town, the friars were valued for their preaching and for their work with the poor. In many places the friaries were in debt and demoralised, but in Dorchester they possessed mills along the banks of the River Frome, and enjoyed a reasonable income. They ran a school and managed an almshouse, and townspeople continued to leave bequests to the friary in their wills. Even William Middleton, who was abbot of Milton for 43 years from 1482-1525, left a legacy to the friars of Dorchester. Unlike monks and nuns, the friars received no pensions from the Crown, so that it is difficult to follow their subsequent careers. We do know that at Dorchester Dr William Germen became vicar of Holy Trinity; the friary church was demolished and the friary buildings were converted into a fine house.

Meanwhile, one by one the Dorset monasteries succumbed to pressure and surrendered during the early spring of 1539 to the King's commissioner, John Tregonwell. Almost the last to yield to the royal will was the ancient nunnery at Shaftesbury on 23 March 1539. The nuns were evidently very reluctant to abandon their way of life and in December 1538 they had persuaded the royal commissioner, Thomas Arundell, to write to Cromwell on their behalf: '. . . they have most heartily desired me to write unto your good Lordship to move their petition . . . that they may remain here . . . for the which they would gladly give unto his said Majesty five hundred marks, and unto your

Lordship for your pains one hundred pounds'.

He added that the abbot and monks of Cerne had made a similar offer. Such pleas counted for little against the prospect of the Crown obtaining all the lands and property which the abbeys had acquired over the centuries. The Augustinian house at Christchurch (which was then in Hampshire) held out until December 1539. The last prior, John Draper, made a passionate appeal that the house should be allowed to continue on the grounds that it not only supported 'poor religious men' but also that the priory church was used for worship by 1,500 people from the town and surrounding hamlets. It also provided extensive charity: '. . . the poor not only of the parish and town but also of the country, were daily relieved and sustained with bread and ale, purposely baked and brewed for them weekly to no small quantities'.

The prior's pleas were in vain, and the house was suppressed, but in October 1540 the church was granted to the town as its parish church.

The dissolution of the monasteries was followed by a scramble among the local gentry, royal servants and wealthy merchants to secure parts of the former monastic sites, buildings and lands. Those who were successful had long been involved with the administration of the estates of the abbeys or had acted as royal commissioners for Thomas Cromwell. Sir John Horsey of Clifton Maybank, who was to obtain much of Sherborne Abbey estates, had been involved with the affairs of the abbey since long before the Dissolution. By offering a large bribe to Thomas Cromwell he had ensured that one of the monks, John Barnstaple, was elected as abbot in 1535. Barnstaple was known to be ready to co-operate with any plan for dissolution, and in 1539 he was rewarded with a large pension and became rector of Stalbridge, and Sir John Horsey obtained the site, buildings and lands of the abbey. Sir John Tregonwell, who acquired Milton Abbey, had spent many years in the royal service. Sir Thomas Arundell came from a wealthy Cornish family which was to remain staunchly Catholic. During the fifteenth century they had acquired Chideock Castle and estates in west Dorset. Thomas Arundell had loyally served Cromwell as a commissioner and was now rewarded by the acquisition of vast estates belonging to the nuns of Shaftesbury. By 1550 Arundell had

An eighteenth century view of the ruins of Chideock Castle. Nothing now remains of this late-medieval castle which was once part of the vast possessions of the Arundell family.

over-reached himself, and found himself on the wrong side in the changing religious and political scene during the reign of Edward VI. Because of his Catholicism and support for the Cornish rebels in 1549 he was executed in 1552, and his estates were forfeit to the Crown; they were, however, restored to his widow and son, Matthew, during Mary's reign, and the Arundell castles at Wardour and Chideock remained bastions of the Catholic faith through all the subsequent persecutions.

The new owners of Dorset's religious houses wasted no opportunity to recoup their investment. The monastery churches at Shaftesbury, Abbotsbury and Cerne were rapidly destroyed. Sherborne was sold to the parishioners by Sir John Horsey and became their parish church in place of the adjacent church of All Hallows' which was demolished. The monastic buildings at Milton became the elegant mansion of Sir John Tregonwell, those at Forde were converted into a dwelling by Richard Pollard, another of the royal commissioners who quickly demolished the church. The lead from the roofs was particularly valuable and was soon sold by the new owners. The buildings themselves became a ready source of good-quality cut stone and were used as quarries. In this process innumerable fine carvings, statues, windows and artistic treasures, as well as the monastic libraries, were destroyed or dispersed. Already in 1548 a survey of the property of

A view of the gateway to the abbot's hall at Cerne Abbas. It survived the destruction of the abbey by being converted into a dwelling.

Shaftesbury showed that the nunnery and its church had been demolished, the lead had been removed from the roofs and all was in ruins. Soon afterwards, evidence in a legal suit over the site of Cerne Abbey, revealed that most of the buildings were demolished, the lead had been sold and great quantities of stone had been carried away 'by gentlemen of the county'. The gatehouse at Cerne, part of which survives, escaped destruction by being turned into a dwelling, and the abbey guest-house also remains, but all other buildings have vanished.

Pensions were provided for the former monks and nuns, no doubt as an inducement to surrender. Some monks obtained positions as parish priests or chantry chaplains, whilst the former heads of houses were able to live comfortably and in some style on their pensions. An example is Margaret Russell, the former abbess of the Cistercian nunnery at Tarrant Crawford. She was awarded a pension of £40 per annum, and moved to Bere Regis where she lived in a manner befitting her position as a cousin of the Duke of Bedford. When she died in 1568 she left a quantity of silver plate, cups, chalices, cruets, rings, valuable furnishings and a remarkable collection of colourful, fashionable clothes, far removed from her former sombre habit as a nun. She had obviously devoted her time to needlework, and her house was filled with embroidered cushions, pillows and coverlets.

Also affected by the Dissolution were the numerous lay servants formerly employed in the monasteries. Most of these were instantly dismissed when the houses were suppressed. For example, the aristocratic nuns at Shaftesbury employed a large number of local people in their kitchens, stables, laundry, workshops and brewery. All of these workers lost their jobs when the nunnery was dissolved. In Dorset, as throughout the south, the suppression of the ancient abbeys provoked no resistance or protest. The effects were, however, felt throughout the county, with the cessation of monastic charity, the disappearance of employment and new landlords keen to make profits from their newly-acquired lands.

In 1542 Dorset suffered another major upheaval in its ecclesiastical organisation. In the wake of the Dissolution, Henry VIII resolved to create six new dioceses, one of them for the busy port of Bristol – previously part of the diocese of Worcester. Bristol alone was considered too small to warrant a diocese, and in a plan evidently designed by an official in London, unaware of West Country geography, it was decided that Dorset should be moved from the diocese of Salisbury and become part of the new diocese of Bristol. This highly-inconvenient arrangement was to last until another major re-organisation was carried out in 1836.

Apart from the introduction of the bible in English in 1538 and a Litany in English in 1545, few other changes in parish worship took place during Henry VIII's reign, the Latin Mass continued, as did the old order of festivals, ceremonies, processions and ritual. With the accession in 1547 of the nine-year old Edward VI, came an avalanche of change which destroyed the doctrines, worship and established routines of parish life. In 1547 chantries and religious guilds were abolished and all their possessions were seized by the Crown. The next few years saw the transformation of the interior appearance of parish churches as images, wall-paintings, figures of the saints, stained glass, screens and crucifixes were torn down, obliterated or destroyed. The ancient Latin mass was abolished and replaced by services in English from a Book of Common Prayer issued in 1549. Throughout Dorset

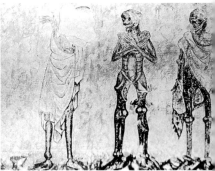

Wall paintings like these, from the nave of Tarrant Crawford church , are rare survivals: most were destroyed or painted over following the Reformation. Those at Tarrant Crawford were uncovered during restoration in 1910. and the ones illustrated here depict the meeting between three kings out hunting and three corpses, together with the moralistic warning, 'As you are so were we, as we are so shall you be'.

there were many chantries, mostly within existing churches, which had been endowed by their founders with lands and property, now all were suppressed. At Wimborne Minster, for example, where the regular round of services conducted by the College of Canons had so far been undisturbed, the abolition of chantries in 1547 led to the suppression of the College. The ten stone altars in the church were demolished, the plate and valuables were sold and the religious paintings on the walls were covered with whitewash. The chantry of the Hospital of St Margaret and St Anthony was suppressed and the management of the hospital or almshouse was vested in two elected parishioners. The grammar school managed to survive to be re-founded by Queen Elizabeth in 1563.

By 1552 the new, simple form of worship ordered by the Book of Common Prayer of 1549, was replaced by an even more Protestant version. This made much of the plate, vestments, altar frontals and other valuables in each parish church unnecessary. Almost everything was confiscated by the Crown, leaving only the bare minimum for the services. The scale of the confiscations and the way in which the government seized the best and most valuable items can be seen from the following examples: St Mary's, Wareham, possessed an impressive collection of silver chalices, crosses, censers, paxes, embroidered vestments and four bells in the tower; the commissioners appointed by the Crown allowed the parish to keep one chalice, one cope and the clothes for the altar. Everything else was confiscated. Milton Abbas had an even larger amount of silver and brass plate, and a multitude of silk and satin vestments; the church was allowed to keep 'the worst chalis, 1 cope of whyt Damask, with all the Table clothes and surplices', the rest was seized by the Crown. At Hazelbury Bryan the church possessed two silver chalices, a silver 'pyx' or receptacle for the Sacrament, a brass censer and other brass items, numerous suits of vestments, altar frontals and 5 bells in the tower; all was confiscated except 'the worst chalice, one cope, one surplice and a table cloth'.

Throughout Dorset similar confiscations occurred, and the churches were allowed to keep 'the worst' chalice and one vestment for the priest. All these changes and confiscations were accepted in Dorset without any open protest. Even more remarkable was the absence of any dissent when Edward VI was succeeded in 1553 by his half-sister Mary who immediately restored Catholicism and the Latin mass. Many items which had recently been confiscated or destroyed had to be replaced at great cost to each parish. A few of the Dorset clergy resigned rather than accept the restoration of Catholicism, or were expelled because they had married during Edward VI's reign, but most conformed, perhaps happy to accept a return to the old, familiar regime and services to which they had been long accustomed.

Among those who resigned was Thomas Hancock of Poole, a fervent supporter of reform in the church and a fiery preacher, who welcomed the changes of Edward's reign and only regretted that they were not more radical. He relates that during the reign of 'good King Edward' he had great success 'in preaching of God's word in the towne of Poole', and adds that 'they were the first thatt in thatt parte of England were called Protestantes'. When Mary succeeded and 'the Mass and other superstitious ceremonies' were restored, he preached vehemently against the change at great risk to his life. Eventually, in 1554 he was persuaded 'for saveguard of my lyfe too flee' to continental Europe, only returning when Mary died in 1558.

# ELIZABETHAN DORSET

The suppression of the monasteries and the dispersal of their vast estates by Queen Elizabeth's father, Henry VIII, resulted in a massive redistribution of land on a scale not seen since the wholesale transfers following the Norman Conquest. The arrival of aggressive and energetic new owners, keen to profit from their acquisitions and establish their position within the county, had a profound effect on the landscape, farming and government of Dorset. Of the 211 leading families in Dorset at the end of Elizabeth's reign in 1603, nearly half the total appeared for the first time in the ranks of the gentry during the sixteenth century. The perceptive local commentator, Thomas Gerard, noted the increased prosperity and the number of men 'who now beginne to encroach upon the Gentrie', and the Devon author, John Hooker, was impressed by the number of lawyers, merchants and yeomen 'clymbying uppe daylye to the degree of Gentleman'.

An example of the sort of 'new men' who rose to wealth and status in the county was Sir John Tregonwell. Despite being a Catholic, his assiduous service to the Crown was eventually rewarded by the opportunity to purchase the lands and buildings of Milton Abbey, worth £666 per annum for the bargain price of £1,000. He turned the former monastic buildings at Milton into a fine mansion, and established his family there in great style with numerous servants and retainers, including '30 gentlemen or yeomen over and besides those who daily attend him in his household or serve him in any office'. He was knighted by Queen Mary at her coronation, and on his death in 1565 he was buried in the former abbey church at Milton beneath a Catholic-style altar tomb and with a traditional Catholic inscription invoking prayers for his soul.

An example of the way in which new landowners endeavoured to exploit the resources of their estates occurred on the large manor of Canford, which stretched along the eastern shores of Poole Harbour

The brass memorial to Sir John Tregonwell (d.1565) in Milton Abbey. In spite of his involvement in the dissolution of the monasteries, he retained his Catholic faith and is buried under a traditional altar tomb. The choughs are a reminder of his Cornish origin.

and inland across the heath almost to Wimborne Minster. Early in Queen Elizabeth's reign much of this area was inherited by James Blount, Lord Mountjoy, who immediately began an energetic quest to profit from the alum and copperas which were found there (*see the plan on page 7*). Alum was in great demand as an important mordant in the dyeing of cloth and was used by tanners; large amounts were annually imported from southern France. Copperas (iron sulphate) was also used by dyers and in the manufacture of ink. Mountjoy spent large sums of money on the complex process of producing alum, and although some saleable quantities were made, these were insufficient to cover the heavy costs of production.

   The production of copperas in Dorset incidentally gave rise to a remarkable Elizabethan 'scam', illustrating the gullibility even of apparently clear-headed statesmen. A young adventurer, William Medley, managed to persuade the Elizabethan lawyer and statesman, Sir Thomas Smith, that copper could be produced from iron through the use of copperas. A cheap new source of copper was a tempting prospect, and Sir Thomas Smith induced prominent astute figures such as William Cecil, later Lord Burghley, Robert Dudley, Earl of Leicester and Humphrey Gilbert to invest large sums in the enterprise. A mine at Canford was leased for £400 per annum to supply the necessary copperas, and large sums were advanced to Medley so that he could go ahead with the process of transmutation. Only after several years and the payment of much money was it realised that Medley was a rogue, the hope of producing copper was a myth and the speculators would not get any return on their investment. The project was abandoned, Medley was declared bankrupt and imprisoned.

Another entrepreneur was Sir William Clavell of Smedmore (1568-1644), although sadly his attempts to exploit the natural resources of his estate all ended in failure. His projects included alum and copperas production, glass-smelting and salt boiling, using the oil-bearing shale from the cliffs at Kimmeridge. His enterprises fell foul of various government monopolies, and eventually he was obliged to sell much of his land to pay his debts, leaving only the remnants of his pier and the wreckage of his glass furnaces as a memorial to his endeavours.

Most landowners adopted the slower but surer method of profiting from their lands by encouraging the spread of improved farming methods, often at the expense of their tenants, or by enclosures. At Iwerne Courtney, which belonged to the earls of Devon, a survey of the manor conducted in 1553 records that the lands were formerly in common, but that in 1548 the tenants had agreed among themselves and with the lord of the manor to enclose the land into separate holdings:

'The custumarye tenaunts were so small and so lyttle londe longinge to them that the tenaunts were not able to paye the lordes rent, but the one halfe of them departed the towne, and yielded up ther copies into the lordes handes; . . . .and then every tenaunte inclosed his owne londes, so as the more parte of t'hole mannor was inclosed, and every tenaunt and fermor occupyed his grounde severall to hymself.'

The sixteenth century saw a massive expansion of sheep flocks at the expense of arable land. This was the period when the huge flocks which were remarked upon by all later travellers in the county made their appearance. At Wimborne St Giles the energetic landowner, Sir Anthony Ashley, was able to put pressure on his tenants to agree to a division and enclosure of the sheep downs by threatening that if they resisted he would greatly increase the size of his own sheep flock and would extend his rabbit warren. The depopulation which followed is apparent from the numerous declined or deserted settlements in the surrounding area. The Provost and Fellows of King's College, Cambridge were able to force their tenants at Stour Provost to accept a proposal for enclosing 1,300 acres of common grazing land by threatening to involve them in an expensive legal suit if they refused. The result can be still be seen in the landscape, where regular square fields replaced the common land and the boundaries of other fields follow the curving lines of the former arable strips.

Early in the seventeenth century, Mervyn, Lord Audley, Earl of Castlehaven, purchased the manor of Stalbridge and began building a large mansion, extending his park to include 'a great pasture and waste and wooddy ground'. This had traditionally been used by the tenants at Stalbridge as grazing land and for cutting fuel. They brought a suit against the earl in the Court of Chancery, but were forced to abandon their claim because of rapidly-mounting legal costs. The result of their failure is still apparent in the great five mile long wall which encloses the park. The earl himself was later executed for a series of bestial crimes, including rape.

Other landowners introduced the cultivation of new and profitable crops. The Strode family of Parnham greatly encouraged the growth of hemp and flax, which was the basis of the rope, twine, net and sailcloth industry of west Dorset and which had previously been imported. The cultivation of woad was introduced on Cranborne Chase and at Sturminster Marshall to replace imported supplies. Woad was the basis of all dark dyes for cloth. The Salisbury lawyer, Henry Sherfield, the wealthy clothier George Bedford and other dyers and cloth workers leased virgin land, parts of former deer parks and rabbit warrens for the cultivation of this hungry and labour-intensive crop. The cultivation of hops was also introduced, especially around towns which were to remain famous for the quality of their beer, such as Dorchester, Cerne Abbas and Blandford Forum.

The rise of the new families is marked by their ornate tombs, memorials and family pews in the parish churches. Tombs such as those of the Frekes at Iwerne Courtney, the Strangways at Melbury, the Winstons at Long Burton (see following page), the Martyns at Puddletown, the Horseys at Sherborne and the Ashleys at Wimborne St Giles leave no doubt of their aggressive assertion of leadership in the local community. The aspiration of the rising gentry families is also evident from the multitude of beautiful manor houses which they built, and which remain as such a characteristic feature of the Dorset landscape. Examples include the mansion at Clifton Maybank near

Part of the large monument in Long Burton church to Sir Thomas Winston and his wife erected in 1609, overwhelming the small parish church.

Sherborne built by Sir John Horsey in about 1560, the Elizabethan manor house at Tyneham, Herringston south of Dorchester built by the Williams family, Edmondsham House of 1589 and Sir Walter Raleigh's Lodge or Castle at Sherborne. Later houses include Hanford House built by Sir Robert Seymer during 1604-23; Up Cerne built by Sir Robert Mellor who died in 1624; Sir John Strode's Chantmarle in 1612; and the elegant house at Winterborne Anderson built by Sir John Tregonwell in 1622.

The former manor house at Tyneham, largely dating from the sixteenth century. The house and village were commandeered for military training during the Second World War, and the house is now a ruin.

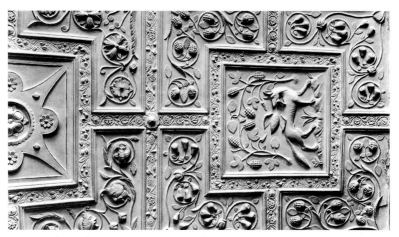

Detail of the plaster-work ceiling decoration of about 1612 from the Great Chamber of Sir John William's mansion at Winterborne Herringston. There are flowers and fruit and, in the central panel, a fox carrying a goose. Such fine work is an indication of the increasing wealth and sophistication of Dorset's gentry families.

Edmondsham House. The central gable bears the date 1589, and above the door are the arms of the Hussey family: the wings are Georgian additions. Only a year earlier, Thomas Hussey had been one of the leaders of the Dorset horsemen at the time of the Armada.

*Above left* The charming brass memorial to Mary Argenton (d.1616) in Woolland church.

*Above right* A romantic representation of Thomas Pilchard, the Catholic priest who suffered an agonising death at Dorchester in 1584.

Many of the Dorset Elizabethan gentry were linked by ties of marriage or family relationship. A charming brass memorial in Woolland church on the slopes of Bulbarrow Hill illustrates these links. It commemorates a widow, Mary Argenton, lady of the manor of Woolland, who is described as 'our Landladie'. She was the sister of Sir John Williams of Herringston and had previously married into the ancient and wealthy Dorset family of Thornhill. Her lineage and relationships were, therefore, impeccable, she was evidently rich, and was said to possess the additional virtues of being charitable and pious. A long eulogy on her memorial emphasises all these qualities, and concludes:

> 'Then rest we assured through God's good grace
> Her soule in the heavens hath taken her place.'

Under Queen Elizabeth England was returned to the Protestant side in the great struggle which now divided the whole of Europe. The result was that in Dorset, as throughout England, Elizabeth's long reign was disrupted by the bitter dissatisfaction of two religious groups. The rapidly-growing Puritan faction wished to see much more reform in the Church, whilst a sizeable minority remained loyal to the old religion and steadfastly refused to abandon Catholicism, in spite of government pressure and growing persecution.

The Catholics in Dorset included some of the oldest and most influential families in the county, including the Turbervilles of Bere Regis, the Martyns of Athelhampton, the Stourtons of Canford, the Tregonwells of Milton Abbas and the Arundells of Chideock. They were able to sustain groups of Catholics among their tenants and neighbours throughout the later sixteenth century. Most of the Catholic priests executed in the county had been chaplains at Chideock for the Arundells or were arrested while being given shelter there. The most notable was Blessed John Cornelius, who spent eleven years in England at various Arundell houses in Cornwall, Dorset, London and elsewhere converting, strengthening and encouraging the Catholic laity. For a time was kept prisoner at Sir George Trenchard's house at Wolfeton, where he disputed with many Dorset notables, including Sir Walter Raleigh, leaving a deep impression on those who spoke with him. Subsequently he was tried, found guilty of treason and executed at Dorchester in July 1594.

Other Catholics from Dorset who died for their faith during Elizabeth's reign included John Mundyn of Mapperton, a schoolmaster who was executed in London in 1584. Another priest, Thomas Pilchard, was executed at Dorchester in 1584, and a layman, William Pike from Parley, a joiner by trade, was executed at Dorchester in 1591. These are a few of the men who, in Dorset as elsewhere, found themselves implicated in a web of religion, international diplomacy and fear of foreign invasion or of popular insurrection and suffered in consequence.

Dorset also had the curious distinction, during the reign of Elizabeth, of producing the man who, perhaps more than any other, was responsible for bringing Mary, Queen of Scots, to the block. He was Arthur Gregory of Lyme Regis who in Fuller's words, 'had the art of forcing the seal of a letter; yet so invisibly, that it still appeared a virgin to the exactest beholder'. He was employed by Walsingham to open the Queen of Scots' letters and thus secure details of the Babington Plot.

The growing strength of Puritanism led to many successful attempts to suppress traditional games, sports, May Day customs and other activities which were regarded as frivolous and leading to drunkeness, disorder and neglect of church-going. At Weymouth there were objections to May games, where the custom was 'to electe and chuse one of the said Inhabitants to be Robin Hoode and another Lyttel John'. Similar pastimes occurred 'in divers towns and villages within the county of Dorset in spring tyme'. Gillingham had revels which revolved around a 'Cuckoo King'. At Lyme Regis Puritan townsmen disapproved of the ancient Easter and Whitsuntide processions to the Cobb, 'which wee take to be a profane use contrary to the right Sanctity of the Lord's Day'. There were complaints from Fordington, Wimborne, Bridport and other Puritan strongholds about games being played in churchyards, about the Shrove Tuesday games at Corfe Castle, and at Marnhull and Piddlehinton there were calls to abandon the ancient practice of distributing bread, cheese and beer in the church on Easter Sunday.

The return to Protestantism under Elizabeth led inevitably to conflict with Spain. Fear and hatred of Catholicism was strengthened in 1568 by the arrival of Mary, Queen of Scots in England, by rumours of successive plots against Queen Elizabeth, and by the execution of Mary in 1587, leading to the Spanish Armada in 1588. The Dorset coastal defences were strengthened to meet a possible invasion and inland towns were made ready to resist invaders. The militias were mustered and trained, beacons were set up along the coast and on inland hill-tops, bridges were guarded and all strangers regarded with the utmost suspicion. Although the imminent approach of the Armada was well known, no-one knew if, when or where an invasion would occur, and the whole county was fearful. Even at inland Sherborne, farmers refused to complete bargains at the market because of the uncertainty of invasion. In the event, the Armada sailed on up the English Channel, but a spectacular sea-battle was fought off Portland on 2 August 1588. The Spanish fleet was becalmed as it neared Portland Bill on the evening of Monday 1 August, and on the following day a fierce engagement took place between the Armada and the English ships. The battle was fought close to the land and was clearly visible to watchers on the coast. Martin Frobisher, commanding the *Triumph*, the largest ship in either fleet, cleverly made use of his knowledge of the coast by anchoring in the lee of Portland Bill from where he was able to inflict considerable damage on the Spanish ships, which were exposed both to fire from the

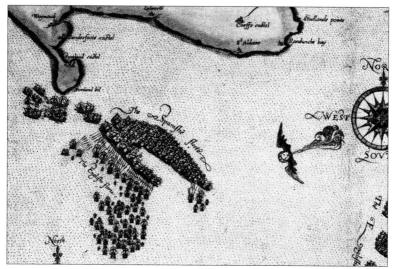

A contemporary view of the Battle of Portland on August 2, 1588.
Frobisher's *Triumph* is amongst the group of English ships off Portland Bill.

English and to the navigational perils of the Portland Race and the Shambles sand bank.

Apart from farming, it was the cloth industry which provided work for many people living in Elizabethan Dorset. Dorchester was said to 'gaine much by Clothage and altogether trade in merchandize, Weymouth being soe neare a Neighbour unto them'. Evidence of the scale of production occurs in 1574 when Richard Criche of Gillingham, clothier, complained to the Court of Requests that he had not received payment for a consignment of cloth sent to a London merchant worth £301 10s 0d. Some of the cloth produced in Dorset was not the high-quality broadcloth, but inferior kersies and 'Dorset dozens', which were much cheaper. Lyme Regis had a considerable trade in lower-quality cloth with Brittany and Normandy, where it was said the people 'are poore and of a base disposition and will not go to the price of a good cloth'.

Many Dorset mills were used both for fulling cloth and for grinding corn. Manorial custom generally required tenants to have their corn ground at the manorial mill, and this obligation was often much resented. In return for his work, the miller was entitled to take a toll from the corn he had ground, and this provided opportunities for fraud. Manorial court rolls contain many references to disputes over mills, and at Chideock, for example, the miller was obliged to produce his 'toll dish' at every meeting of the manorial court. The strained relationship between millers and their customers is reflected in the verse carved on the mill at Fiddleford in Sturminster Newton parish, which is dated 1566. This warns the miller against dishonesty and ends with the exhortation:

'Therefore to be true yt shall thee behove
[To] please god chefly [that liveth] above'.

Fishing continued to be important at ports along the coast, and especially at Poole, although in addition to its obvious dangers, the lure of a large and lucrative catch could lead to the neglect of other, surer occupations. A survey of Long Bredy noted 'this manor lyinge so near to the sea becomes the lesse manured and the worse husbanded for that they follow fishing and leave theire husbandrye, especially in pilchard time'. At West Lulworth, however, the surveyor commented 'the Tennants make greate Profitt by Fishinge'.

One hazard to trade was pirates, who were especially numerous around Purbeck, from where they attacked ships from Poole. Their operation, like those of smugglers, was protected through the powerful influence of landowners such as Sir Richard Rogers of Bryanston, Henry Howard of Bindon, Francis Hawley of Corfe Castle and merchants such as Robert Gregory of Weymouth. The fact that Poole had been granted county status in 1568 was an additional complication. In one campaign against piracy, in 1581, a pirate ship was captured in Studland Bay, and a notorious pirate, John Piers of Padstow in Cornwall, and several of his companions were imprisoned at Dorchester. After they were tried and sentenced to be hanged, an instruction from the Privy Council ordered that they 'be executed at Studland to the terryfying of others, for that the same place hathe beene muche frequented and the inhabitants molested with pirates'. From time to time other pirates were executed, but the twin problems of piracy and smuggling were to continue throughout the later sixteenth century and beyond.

# THE EARLY STUART PERIOD

Under James I and his son, Charles I, tensions and divisions in Dorset society increased rapidly, as they did throughout England, eventually culminating in armed rebellion and civil war. The period was one of unprecedented political controversy, fanned by the profound loathing for Catholicism and Spain. Social tensions in Dorset were exacerbated by a rapid increase in population and a growing problem of unemployment, poverty, vagrancy and lawlessness.

Although precise figures are lacking, it is clear that between 1500 and 1650 the population of Dorset more than doubled; Dorchester, for example, grew from about 1000 to 2500. Since Dorset was predominately an agricultural county and the demand for farm labour fluctuated greatly throughout the year, there was inevitably a great deal of unemployment and consequent poverty. It was landless labourers with nowhere to live who created the poor cottages or

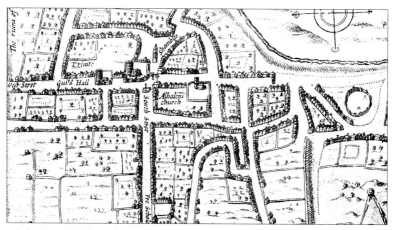

John Speed's plan of Dorchester in 1610, showing the three churches, the houses along the main streets and the large areas of open ground remaining with the Roman walls of the town.

If any one person can be said to mirror the flawed brilliance of the late Elizabethan and early Stuart times then it is surely Sir Walter Raleigh (1552-1618), shown here in the 'miniature' by Nicholas Hilliard. He acquired the old castle at Sherborne in 1592 and built the new castle nearby. It was there that he spent some of the happiest time of his turbulent life.

hovels on waste ground which are frequently mentioned and complained about in parish and manorial records of the early seventeenth century. For example, at Netherbury in 1626 the parishioners complained:

> 'there are nowe Latelie erected eight or ten poore Cottages on which divers poore people dwell and . . . they take liberty to themselves to keep unlicensed alehouses and have divers disorderlie meetings where (it is feared) manie stollen goods are consumed to the greate griefe and losse of theire honest neighbours.'

Similar complaints came from the woodland areas of the Blackmore Vale and Cranborne Chase, and from the heathland of east Dorset. At Holnest in 1630 the inhabitants complained to the justices in Quarter Sessions that

> 'divers boyes, young men and unmarried persons have by the Tilemakers and Brickmakers, Potters and others within the parish of Holnest . . . been brought in to the said parish to worke at dayes labour . . . who do live loosely, frequenting alehouses and committing many disorders'.

At Kingston Lacy where there was some employment in digging clay for bricks, tiles and pottery, 35 unauthorised and newly-erected dwellings were listed in a survey of 1591. The flimsy nature of these structures, often set up overnight in the widespread but erroneous belief that this conferred squatters' rights, can be seen from an example at Cranborne in 1625 where the residents complained that 'Richard Cooke intends either this night or the next to set up a house (which he hath already framed) and hath placed straw upon the common in the place he hath made choyce of to erect his house in'. At Cerne Abbas, a survey of 1617 revealed that many of the houses were occupied by 'a masse of base people, meer mendicantes (beggars)'. The surveyor noted that, for example, 'John Williams hath a fayer house and hath put neer a dozen lowsy people in it'.

There were great contrasts in society, and extreme poverty existed alongside great wealth. Many gentry families had prospered from the demand for wool and cloth, and lawyers and merchants had become sufficiently wealthy to acquire country estates. Following the execution of Sir Walter Raleigh in 1618 and the confiscation of his Sherborne estate by the Crown, the property, including Raleigh's new mansion, was granted to Sir John Digby who had been James I's ambassador to Spain. In 1641 the Lulworth estate of the Earls of Suffolk, together with the picturesque 'Castle' or hunting-lodge built with material from nearby Bindon Abbey, was purchased by Humphrey Weld, a wealthy London merchant.

Lulworth Castle was originally built as a hunting-lodge using material from Bindon Abbey by Thomas Howard, Lord Bindon, during the early seventeenth century. It was gutted by fire in 1929 and only a shell survives.

Chantmarle, near Cattistock, built by the lawyer Sir John Strode in about 1612. The estate had been owned since early Tudor times by the Cheverell family, but they had been forced to sell up in 1606, and Chantmarle is a fine example of the way in which new money, made in London, was gradually ousting the old – something that continues into the present.

The wealth and opulent life-style of the Dorset gentry families is evident from the remarkable number of seventeenth-century manor houses which remain all across the county. The beautiful manor house at Chantmarle, near Cattistock, was built in about 1612 at a cost of £1,142 by Sir John Strode, a lawyer and younger son of the family at Parnham. His account book records in detail the entire cost and process of building, using stone from the quarries at Ham Hill in south Somerset. Strongly Puritan in his religious views, Sir John Strode emphasised that his house was built in the form of an E to represent the word EMMANUEL, which is carved on the keystone of the porch and which he explained was to mean 'God with us in Eternity'. Included in the building was a splendid chapel with a plaster ceiling, 'fretted over with the sun, moon, starrs, cherubims, doves, grapes and pomegranates, all supported with 4 angells in the 4 corners of the roofe'.

A large expanse of Cranborne Chase was granted to James I's chief minister, Robert Cecil, Earl of Salisbury, who remodelled the medieval house at Cranborne in a suitably lavish style, creating one of the loveliest of all Dorset manor houses. The building work was

*Above left*  Robert Cecil, 1st Earl of Salisbury (1563-1612), who acquired the estate at Cranborne where he rebuilt the former royal hunting lodge. He was the leading figure in government during the early years of James I, and entertained the king and his Court at Cranborne on several occasions.

*Above right*  Cranborne Manor as expensively re-fashioned by Robert Cecil.

supervised by William Arnold, a well-known architect from Somerset, and the gardens were laid out by the Hatfield gardener, John Tradescant. Vast sums were spent, even though Hatfield House in Hertfordshire was the Earl's main residence. One purpose of the manor house was to provide suitable accommodation for James I when he hunted on Cranborne Chase. One visit in August 1618 is recorded in detail in the Earl of Salisbury's account book. The total cost of entertaining the royal party came to £405 19s 0d, and included the consumption of 3 bullocks, 48 sheep, 20 calves, innumerable ducks, turkeys, capons and pheasants, as well as 250 gallons of claret, 28 gallons of sack, 41 gallons of white wine and an amazing 1,750 gallons of beer. Accompanying the King was a small army of courtiers, servants, cooks, grooms and huntsmen, many of whom were lodged in farmhouses and cottages around Cranborne. Evidence of the effect of this crowd of Londoners upon a quiet corner of Dorset is provided by the court records which show numerous charges of assault, robbery, violence and drunkeness in the area during the royal visit. For example, three grooms 'attendant on Sir Archibald Napper, knight and Sir John Wood, knight', were arrested for fighting and wounding another servant by stabbing him with a knife. Their duties had consisted in guiding the two knights from Cranborne 'with a Torch unto their lodging at the farme of Mr Thomas Hooper called the New Barne'.

An example of a lawyer who rose to great wealth and influence in Dorset is Sir Francis Ashley (1569-1635), Reader in Law at the Middle Temple and Recorder of Dorchester. He was a member of the Ashley, later Ashley-Cooper, family established at Wimborne St Giles since the reign of Henry VI. Becoming a barrister, Francis Ashley built up a lucrative practice in London, and in 1610 was appointed Recorder or borough magistrate of Dorchester. He married the daughter of Bernard Samways of Toller Fratrum, and through her acquired land and property at Winterborne St Martin. He lived in the former friary building by the side of the River Frome in Dorchester and, whilst maintaining his London practice, became an active magistrate in Dorset, representing Dorchester in the parliaments of 1614, 1621 and 1625-6. In Dorchester he was greatly influenced by the powerful preaching of the rector, John White, and became an active Puritan. He was involved with John White's schemes to send parties from Dorset to New England. Francis Ashley's only daughter, Dorothy, married Denzil Holles, a son of the Earl of Clare. Holles later represented Dorchester in Parliament and was a prominent critic of Charles I.

During his time as a magistrate, Francis Ashley kept a case book or notes on the cases which came before him. Particularly revealing are the numerous vagabonds, thieves, pick-pockets and tricksters who were brought before him each year, having been arrested at Woodbury Hill Fair. The three-day fair was held in September each year on a hill-top near Bere Regis, and attracted buyers and sellers from long distances. The local influence of the fair was such that in 1648 a public thanksgiving in Dorchester was postponed because 'it falls out to be on Woodbury Fair Eve, at which time most of the town will be from home'. The evidence given by witnesses in the cases brought before Ashley mentions the crowds, the sellers of food and ale, butter, cheese, leather goods, cloth, lace and the large numbers of sheep, cattle and horses for sale, as well as the booths, stalls and the tents erected as 'bowers to lodge in for the night'.

Sir Francis Ashley died in November 1635, aged 66. His nephew, Anthony Ashley Cooper, who became the first Earl of Shaftesbury, later accused Sir Francis of trying to acquire part of the Wimborne

Anthony Ashley-Cooper, 1st Earl of Shaftesbury (1621-83), who inherited St Giles House and extensive estates around Wimborne St Giles. 'A dangerous man to deceive,' and a master of intrigue, he was the consummate politician, playing a leading part in national affairs from the time he switched allegiances from king to Parliament during the Cviil War.

estate while he was still a child and a Ward of Court. The Earl claimed that as a young boy he sat powerless while his uncle made 'a long and elegant speech' before the Court of Wards, claiming part of the estate. The boy uttered a silent prayer to be delivered from his uncle's designs upon his inheritance. The result was dramatic, for at that moment Sir Francis collapsed to the floor with a seizure 'his mouth drawn to his ear'. He was carried from the Court, never to speak again, and died a few days later.

Farming in Dorset continued to be divided between the sheep/corn husbandry of the chalklands and the milk, cheese, pigs and fat cattle production of the clay vales in the north and west of the county. Throughout the chalk region the manorial system remained strong; the manorial courts and custom continued to control many aspects of life including land tenure, common-field farming, sheep-grazing and communal relations in the compact villages which are characteristic of this area. In the scattered hamlets and farmsteads of the clay vales manorial control was much weaker, there were fewer common arable fields and much less communal regulation of farming practice.

All farmers were dependent on weekly local markets for the sale of their products and a remarkable picture of the market at Shaftesbury emerges from a legal dispute in 1620 between the corporation of the town and the Earl of Pembroke over the right to levy tolls in the market. Because of its advantageous position midway between the rich lands of the Blackmore Vale and the chalk downlands, Shaftesbury possessed one of the busiest of all the Dorset markets. It was also on the important route from London to the west of England. An indication of its former importance is shown by the number of roads radiating from it to all the surrounding area. The legal dispute reveals the congestion in the town on market days, the pens for sheep and cattle along the streets, the market house near St Peter's church where the town scales and weights were kept, and the corn market with 'a bell to ring when the said market shall begin'. There was a butter cross 'for all those who sold butter, cheese, eggs, poultry or the like to stand or sit dry in during the market'. For the accommodation and refreshment of travellers and market-men there were 24 licensed inns and alehouses in the town.

The period 1600-40 saw major developments and innovation in agriculture. New fodder crops such as cabbages, clover, rye-grass, sainfoin and vetches were introduced. Hemp and flax, the raw materials for the rope, twine, net, sailcloth, canvas and linen industries were increasingly cultivated on the rich clay soils of west Dorset. Thomas Fuller, vicar of Broadwindsor from 1634 to 1641, and the author of *The Worthies of England*, wrote 'England hath no better [hemp] than what groweth here betwixt Beaminster and Bridport'. New developments were eagerly encouraged by landlords keen to improve the rental income from their estates. Thus Sir Thomas Freke of Iwerne Courtney and a group of like-minded gentlemen arranged for an expert on flax and hemp cultivation and processing, Christopher Cockerell, to come to Dorset and demonstrate the techniques, persuading farmers to grow these crops. Another new crop was woad from which a rich blue dye was extracted and used by clothiers and dyers as the basis of all the dark colours. This had been

Thomas Fuller (1608-61) clergyman and historian, author of numerous works, including *The Worthies of England*. He was rector of Broadwindsor 1634-40 and makes many references to west Dorset in his publications.

imported, but from the later sixteenth century it began to be grown in Dorset, notably on a former large deer park and rabbit warren at Blagdon near Cranborne, at Pentridge and at Sturminster Marshall.

Agricultural innovation was also encouraged by Theophilus, Earl of Suffolk, on his 12,000 acre Lulworth estates. His account book records expenditure on drainage projects, including the drainage of Lodmoor on the coast near Weymouth. The division and enclosure of lands at Sutton Poyntz, expansion of his sheep flocks, new crops, orchards, rabbit warrens and garden developments. Drainage and land reclamation was undertaken on Brownsea Island and around the shores of Poole Harbour, although the attempt by a group of gentlemen headed by Sir George Horsey of Clifton Maybank to drain the Fleet, the large area of tidal water between the Chesil Beach and the mainland, ended in disaster. Large sums of money were lost in the abortive effort, and the failure ruined the once-prosperous Horsey family. Sir George was imprisoned for debt in Dorchester gaol and died there.

The most important and far-reaching innovation in Dorset farming, and a major contribution to agricultural progress throughout the country, was the development of water meadows. This involved creating a dam or weir in a chalkland stream and diverting the water along a carefully-constructed series of channels which were made to overflow, so as to cover the surface of a meadow with a thin sheet of moving water. Thus during the winter months the grass could be protected from frost, and was encouraged to grow much earlier than would have occurred naturally. The early grass could be used to feed the sheep flocks; larger flocks could therefore be kept; more arable land could receive the benefit of the sheep fold and much heavier crops of wheat and barley could be produced. Watered again during the early summer, the water meadows produced abundant crops of hay. The fully-advanced technique of controlled watering was unknown before the early seventeenth century and was first developed along the banks of the Frome and Piddle in Dorset.

The earliest reference that has been found anywhere in the country comes from Ilsington near Puddletown in 1608 when four tenants of Henry Arnold were granted leave to construct water courses and channels to bring water from the Frome to water the meadows. Soon afterwards the tenants of Sir Edward Lawrence at Affpuddle were encouraged to combine forces to create water meadows there. By the 1620s water meadows were being developed on the estate of Henry Hastings at Puddletown, and from there the idea quickly spread to nearby manors. The effect of these development was to change the appearance of the Frome and Piddle valleys. Writing in about 1630 the local author, Thomas Gerard, described the Frome as passing 'amongst most Pleasant Meadows manie of which of late yeares have been by Industrie so made of barren Bogges'. From the seventeeth to the early twentieth centuries water meadows were an indispensable feature of chalkland farming, without which the great sheep flocks could not have been maintained, and consequently much less corn could have been grown on thin chalkland soils. This Dorset development proved to be a triumph of English agriculture and the first major breakthrough in the age-old barrier to farming progress.

# POLITICAL AND RELIGIOUS
# CONTROVERSY 1600-1640

Throughout the country, the decades before the Civil War were marked by increasingly acrimonious disputes over religion and politics. Although a sizeable Catholic minority continued to exist in Dorset, protected by a few powerful gentry families, it was Puritan sentiment that grew most strongly in the county. Sherborne had a zealous Puritan minister William Lydford, vicar from 1632 to 1653. The powerful preaching and piety of John White, rector of Holy Trinity, Dorchester from 1605 to 1648, made it one of the most strongly Puritan towns in the whole country. It was John White's preaching which fostered and supported a remarkable attempt to create in Dorchester a god-fearing, benevolent commonwealth, providing care for the sick, education for the young and charity to the poor. Among other schemes was the creation of the Dorchester Company to promote colonization. This was instrumental in founding New Dorchester, Massachusetts in 1630. In Poole, Weymouth, Beaminster and Lyme Regis Puritanism also grew strongly.

Evidence of dissatisfaction with the established church can be seen in the annual reports which the churchwardens of each parish sent to the bishop or other ecclesiastical authorities, and in proceedings in the church courts. In 1617 Richard Holmes of Bloxworth stated that he had called at the house of Christopher Chickerell on a Sunday morning and had found seven or eight people sitting around a table and Chickerell's wife reading a chapter of scripture to them. After the reading they discussed the chapter and its meaning, and they told Holmes that they were 'separatists' and did not agree with the teaching or governance of the church. At Beaminster in 1634 the minister, Mr Spratt, preached hour-long sermons, refused to wear a surplice, to pray for archbishops and bishops, use the Book of

Common Prayer, or follow the orders laid down by the Church. Reports from the churchwardens at Lyme Regis, Charminster, Bloxworth, Stratton, Halstock and Yetminster show a similar revolt from the established practice of the church and refusal to use parts of the liturgy.

The Puritan emphasis on a 'preaching ministry' meant that some of the clergy were criticised for what were considered inadequate sermons. At Over Compton in 1634 a parishioner declared that 'his pigg can write and preach as well as the parson'. Richard Christmas, gentleman, of Sydling St Nicholas set his cat on a post and 'pincht the catt by the ear and made her crye' saying 'he wold make her preach as good a sermon as some of them'. Edward Wills of Hermitage was said to sleep through the services and to make 'unreverent and uncharitable speeches' about the sermons.

It was growing Puritan sentiment which led to the banning of many ancient diversions such as church ales, midsummer revels, Christmas festivities, bowls, skittles, fives and morris dancing. For example, the Wimborne Minster churchwardens regularly reported people for bowling, playing at fives, scandalous or suspicious living, drinking, failure to attend church and fighting. At Fordington in 1631 the churchwardens reported eight people 'for that they have played at a game with a Ball called Fives in the churchyard and they have thereby broken the glasse of one of the windowes of the church'. At Lyme Regis several persons were reported for 'playing at scytels in the churchyard'.

The churchwardens of Frome Whitfield, north of Dorchester, reported in 1606 that 'Mr Henry James, our parson is not resident with us and hath been absent these six years, and there hath been no service in that time. The church is filled up with hay and corne, and is so far in decay that it is like to fall down'. The vicar of Alton Pancras was reproved in 1608 because he went to nearby Cheselbourne 'to footeball upon the Sabbothe day and carried many of his parishioners with him and lost Evening Prayer'. The incumbent of Upwey frequented a local alehouse, and 'was many times so drunk that he had to be carried home and could not read Divine Service on the Sabboth day'.

Serious cases were tried by the church courts. In 1629 William and

Alice Rooklie of Wimborne Minster were sentenced to perform public penance and to confess that after William had made their servant, Mellior Rabbetts pregnant, they had attempted to shift the blame on to the parson, William Gallard, 'against whom [they] heretofore conceived some displeasure'. They were to acknowledge their fault in the parish church at Wimborne Minster immediately after evening prayer 'publicklie before the whole congregation there present'. In a small community such public humiliation must have been a severe ordeal.

The ecclesiastical court records for the seventeenth century also contain many references to witches and witchcraft. Superstitions and the practice of sorcery and magic continued to exercise a hold on the beliefs and imagination of many people living in remote rural communities in Dorset. In 1604, for example Joan Guppy of South Perrott in west Dorset, was accused of witchcraft and of bewitching a neighbour, Margaret Abington. Margaret Abington had lain in wait for Joan Guppy, and had beat her with brambles, intending 'to prick her so as to draw blood' in the belief that this would defeat her power. After drawing blood, Margaret Abington 'found herself much relieved and revived'. Later, Joan Guppy was obliged to produce a certificate signed by several neighbours, stating that she was not a witch, but 'hath donne good to many people as well in Curinge of dyvers people of wounds . . . and in drenching of cattell'. In 1616 Thomas Tyher of Charminster was accused by the churchwardens of witchcraft, casting out devils, administering physic and gaining an unnatural hold over many people in the parish, both men and women.

Seating arrangements within the churches mirrored the rigid social structure of each parish. Many of the pews were rented by their occupants who took the liberty of adapting them to suit their own convenience. This created the sort of problem described by the churchwardens of Preston and Sutton Poyntz in 1638:

'The seate or pew in our church belonging to Mr Robert Mapp and by him formerly erected is offensive to certain persons sitting behind it by reason of the height of it, it standinge a greate deale higher than any seate in the said church, soe those persons that are behind neither see nor well heare the minister reading divine service'.

The social gradations in church seating can still be seen in the

The interior of Chalbury church, showing the box pews.

furnishings of Chalbury and Winterborne Tomson, with the squire's pew in front, box pews for the prosperous farmers, and forms at the back or seats in the west gallery for the labourers and the poor. A positive result of Archbishop Laud's insistence upon improvements to the fabric and furnishings of parish churches, or upon what he described as 'the beauty of holiness', was the addition of new altar rails, pulpits, lecterns and other furnishings in many Dorset churches. Examples of fine seventeenth century pulpits include Chickerell (1630), Charminster (1635), Hammoon (1635), Puddletown (1635), Oborne (1639) and Cerne Abbas (1640). The lofty sounding-board above the pulpit at Lyme Regis leaves no doubt concerning both the donor and his Puritan sentiments:

'To God's Glory Richard Harvey of London
. . . Mercer and Marchant Adventurer 1613
Faith Is By Hearing.'

Any outside source of entertainment was regarded with suspicion, and a chorus of shocked protest greeted a company of puppet-players who travelled through Dorset in 1630. They were turned out of Dorchester, under the powerful influence of the vicar, John White. At Beaminster the townsfolk complained that they could not 'keepe theire Children and Servants in their houses by reason that they frequent the said shewes and sights late in the night in a disorderly manner'. The puppet-players were duly ordered to leave and not return. It says a great deal for the dullness of everyday life in Beaminster that the puppets could cause such havoc in the discipline of children and servants.

The pulpit, St Michael's Church Lyme Regis, given by the Puritan
merchant Richard Harvey in 1613 with an inscription on the
canopy extolling the virtues of the lengthy sermon: 'faith is by hearing'.

The Reformation had abolished almost all the ceremonies,
processions, church ales and revels that had been such a feature of
parish life. One procession did survive. This was the 'beating' or
perambulation of the parish bounds at Rogationtide. Even for this
some parishes gave excuses for neglect of the custom. At Netherbury
in 1613 it was reported that 'new inclosures and multitude of hedges'
made it impossible. At Long Burton in 1625 it was said that 'the
groundes of the parish are soe hedged that we cannot goe'. A major
reason for neglect of the procession was the fact that by custom
certain farms and houses along the route were obliged to provide
refreshment for those taking part, and that householders objected to
the heavy expense of providing the necessary food and drink. On the
chalk downlands where there were few natural landmarks it was
particularly important to maintain knowledge of parish boundaries. A
dispute between the neighbouring parishes of Stratton and
Charminster over the boundary between them reached the Exchequer

The 'Cross in Hand' stone on the escarpment above Batcombe was set up as a boundary marker on the Winchester College estate at Sydling St Nicholas.

Court in 1616. The Stratton men alleged that when a new vicar had arrived at Charminster he was misled by the parishioners in his first Rogationtide procession to 'forsake theire old and wonted way and course', and to extend their boundary into Stratton parish by more than fifty acres of downland grazing. A similar boundary dispute on the high downland overlooking Batcombe was solved by a series of stone posts, one of which is known as the 'Cross in Hand' stone, and has given rise to many legends and superstitions.

The Puritan emphasis on 'good works' is evident from the large number of almshouses, schools and charities endowed in Dorset during the seventeenth century. Among the many examples are Matthew Chubb's foundations at Shaftesbury, Dorchester and Wootton Fitzpaine, Sir Anthony Ashley's almshouses at Wimborne St Giles, Sir Robert Napper's 'Mite' at Dorchester and Sir John Strode's almshouse at Beaminster. Smaller charitable endowments throughout the county are still listed on the Bequest Boards which remain in many parish churches.

Not all the founders of almshouses made their fortunes by totally admirable means. Matthew Chubb of Dorchester had been a rapacious money-lender, charging ιιigh rates of interest and relentlessly pursuing his debtors. There were numerous unavailing complaints about his business methods. Thomas Frye of Chetnole was ruined by Chubb after he had borrowed £100 at 10 per cent interest, and was imprisoned in Dorchester goal. At the time of the great fire in

Sir Anthony Ashley's Almshouses, Wimborne St Giles, founded in 1624.

Dorchester he and other prisoners did valiant work in fire-fighting and afterwards they received a royal pardon for their services. By the time of his death in 1617 Matthew Chubb was extremely rich. His will included a robust statement of his Puritan faith, and his ornate monument in All Saints' church, Dorchester, has the suitably Puritan text: 'Blessed are they which die in the Lord. They rest from their labours, and their works doe follow them'.

The memorial to Matthew Chubb, in All Saints' church, Dorchester.

Growing discontent during the early decades of the seventeenth century over inflation, unemployment, vagrancy, enclosures, rising costs of poor relief and royal taxation, all served to create tensions and divisions among society in Dorset as elsewhere. The practice of 'impressment' or conscription of men and the billeting of soldiers in private houses were both unpopular, and royal taxes, forced loans, monopolies, increased customs duties and especially the new levy known as 'ship-money', were bitterly resented. In Dorset it was reported that in order to pay the royal taxes poor people were forced 'to sell their only cow, which should feed their children', and to seek relief from the parish poor rates.

The mayor and councillors of Weymouth, Melcombe Regis and Poole all claimed that although 'the Inhabitants are full of good will to contribute towards his Majesty's needs', they were unable to do so because of losses of ships and seamen because of the attacks by the Turks in the Mediterranean, the heavy costs of maintaining the wives and children of captured sailors, and the collapse of the trade with Newfoundland.

Dorset members of Parliament frequently complained about the behaviour of soldiers billeted in the county, that they 'disturb markets and fairs, rob men on the highway, ravish women, breaking into houses in the night, with many other offences disrupting the peace'.

It was political tension and dissatisfaction which underlay the major riots which occurred at Gillingham in 1628-30. For generations farmers had enjoyed rights of grazing cattle and pigs in the ancient royal forest of Gillingham. In 1625 the royal forest and many others were 'disafforested' by the Crown in an effort to raise money. A lease of Gillingham forest was granted to Sir James Fullerton, who had been the tutor of Charles I. He proceeded to enclose the forest land, compensating those who claimed rights of grazing with small plots. There was widespread dissatisfaction with the size of the plots, and the commoners attacked Fullerton's servants and tore down the enclosures. This was part of a wider revolt in the former royal forests, and for a time the Gillingham rioters were able to defy the local militia and later the royal troops, declaring in defiance 'Here we were born and here we stay'. Eventually they were overcome by the superior royal forces, the ringleaders were captured and eighty of the rioters were fined. Their defeat was followed by the total enclosure of the former royal forest, but much evidence of its former existence survives in the landscape, including the ruins of the royal hunting lodge on the outskirts of Gillingham.

By 1640 the growing rift between Puritans and Royalists and the entrenched position of both sides meant that the drift to armed conflict would soon become inevitable. When Charles I did finally summon Parliament in 1640 several of the Dorset members were sympathetic to the Puritan and anti-Royalist cause. As well as Denzil Holles, they included Thomas Trenchard of Wolfeton, John Brown of Frampton, who were the county members, Denis Bond of Dorchester (the second member for Dorchester), Edmund Prideaux of Forde Abbey (for Lyme Regis), John Bingham of Bingham's Melcombe (for Shaftesbury), Walter Erle of Charborough (for Weymouth), and Thomas Erle of Charborough (for Wareham). Such men ensured that the King was left in no doubt about the disquiet felt in Dorset at the political, financial and religious policies of the Crown. During the next few months rumours of Catholic plots, of revolts in Scotland over church reform, of growing support for the abolition of bishops and of revolts in Ireland in which Protestants were massacred, all served to increase the apprehension that conflict was becoming inevitable. It was an atmosphere in which a small incident came to be regarded as a major omen. On the day the Long Parliament met on 3 November 1640, a dinner party was held in the Trenchard's great hall at Wolfeton, where the screen contained statues of the monarchs of England. During dinner, the sceptre held by the figure of Charles I suddenly came crashing to the floor.

# CIVIL WAR

When the King raised his standard at Nottingham in August 1642, and when conflict began with the first battle between the royal troops and the Parliamentary forces at Edgehill in October, much of the old loyalty to the Crown among the gentry families of Dorset was re-awakened. Nonetheless, the war sharply divided friends and relatives alike. The majority of large landowners were royalist in sympathy, including the Digbys of Sherborne, the Strangways of Melbury and Abbotsbury, the Bankes of Corfe Castle, the Frekes of Iwerne Courtney and the Turbervilles of Bere Regis. Also royalist were the Catholic families, the Arundells of Chideock, the Tregonwells of Milton and the Welds who had recently purchased Lulworth Castle and its estates.

The inhabitants of many of the Dorset towns and ports were, however, strongly Parliamentarian, particularly Poole, Wareham, Melcombe Regis, Lyme Regis, and Dorchester. As the county town, the seat of the Assizes and the county gaol, and, above all, as the repository of the county militia's supply of ammunition, Dorchester exercised a powerful influence. Later, Clarendon in his magisterial *History of the Rebellion* described Dorchester as 'the magazine from whence the other places were supplied with the principles of Rebellion'.

Dorset played a crucial part in the Civil War, although no major battle was fought in the county. It was strategically important because of its position between the parliamentary headquarters in London and the strongly royalist areas of Devon and Cornwall, and between the royalist stronghold at Oxford and the ports along the Dorset coast which provided contact with France. There were royalist strongholds in the castles at Sherborne, Corfe, Portland and Chideock, and parliamentary garrisons in several towns, especially Poole and Lyme Regis. Early in the conflict much expensive work was undertaken to

The most celebrated casualty of the Civil War in Dorset is Corfe Castle, shown here at the time of the Restoration in 1660 following its destruction by Parliament thirteen years earlier. Mines and large quantities of explosives were used to shatter the defensive walls of the former royal stronghold.

strengthen the defences of towns such as Poole, Wareham, and Lyme. At Dorchester, Maumbury Rings was converted into a gun emplacement controlling the south-west of the town and the road to Weymouth.

During the course of the war the castles at Sherborne and Corfe and the ports of Poole and Lyme Regis suffered long sieges, Weymouth changed hands no less than five times, Beaminster was burnt, Blandford was plundered and taken and retaken four times. Although Lyme Regis and Poole stubbornly resisted the royal forces, much of the rest of the county fell to the Crown during the early months of the war. Even Dorchester, where elaborate and expensive defences had been prepared, surrendered to the royal army without a shot being fired. Royalist soldiers looted John White's house, destroying his library and manuscripts. Lyme Regis was besieged by the royalists for two months in 1644, and suffered an intensive artillery bombardment which did much damage, destroying many houses and leaving few buildings undamaged. In June 1644 a Parliamentary army captured

Weymouth; later in the year Charles I and his army passed through the county after their victorious campaign in the west. There were constant skirmishes between small groups of soldiers from both sides and by 1645 most people in Dorset were heartily sick of the war. At its outbreak the royal manor of Portland had supported the King, but in May 1643 it was taken by Parliamentary troops. The rector of Portland, Dr Humphrey Henchman, an ardent royalist, was ejected and his fine library was destroyed. At the Restoration in 1660 Dr Henchman became bishop of Salisbury and later was created bishop of London. Meanwhile royalist forces in disguise made a surprise attack on Portland and re-captured the Island for the King in August 1643. Thereafter the royalists withstood repeated attacks and valiantly held out until all hope of royal victory was gone in April 1646.

An example of the turmoil created occurred at Wareham. The town, with its good defences, remained royalist until it was taken in a surprise attack in November 1643. It was re-taken by the royalists in April 1644, but surrendered to a Parliamentarian army in July 1644. The royalists took the town once more in February 1646, only to be defeated soon after by the victorious Parliamentary forces engaged on a successful assault on Corfe Castle. Some indication of the effects in the town is shown by the payments authorised by the Parliamentary committee for Dorset. For example, in 1647 Roger Payne was paid £22 for hay, cattle and fat sheep which he supplied to the garrison at Wareham 'for thiere reliefe'. Charles Legg, a fuller, was paid £8 11s 4d for cloth delivered to the garrison, and William Keynell, a barber-surgeon, received £50 for 'divers cures by hime done for wounded souldiers in the towne when it was a garrison for the Parliament'. In addition, there were numerous complaints from those who had suffered losses by requisitioning, quartering of soldiers and plundering.

Similar damage was done to many other towns, A Weymouth merchant complained in 1644 that goods worth more than £1,000 had been stolen from him by soldiers and that because of the war 'noe man could say that anything hee had was his owne'. Another Weymouth merchant buried all his wealth under the floorboards of his house in 1644, but later claimed that soldiers had dug up the floor and removed all except 22s 6d.

Throughout the war, estate accounts from all over the county tell of uncultivated land, destroyed crops and damage to property. The impact of the war upon the helpless farmers and labourers of Dorset is well summarised in heartfelt letters sent to the Earl of Salisbury's steward at Cranborne. In 1645 Allen Winsor who was one of the Earl's tenants at Cranborne explained that he could not pay his rent because

'. . . Sence thes trobls I have left untilled the ground in Blagdon.Besides that which hath benn sowne hath bene much spoyled by solldiers' horses. And that which wee have gotten into our barrn, when any armie have marched neare unto us, wee have suffered much by them'.

Another of the Earl's tenants, John Couridge, who held a three-acre tenement at Tarrant Rushton, explained that he could not pay his rent because he had been forced to provide accommodation for 21 soldiers, he had been obliged to pay 'Contribution money' to the county authorities ever since the War had begun, the soldiers had eaten all his seed corn, and had prevented him from harvesting his crops, he, therefore, hoped that 'my Lord wil be so honourable that he will grant a poor man's request'. Although the Earl was safe from the conflict at Hatfield, he was well aware of the problems since his house at Cranborne had several times been plundered by the soldiers. The worst incident occurred in May 1643 when several hundred troops commanded by Prince Maurice thoroughly sacked the house, stealing what they could and smashing the rest. As later at Corfe Castle and Lulworth, they scattered and destroyed all the estate records they could find. Even the Earl's steward, Samuel Stillingfleet, had to write to Hatfield in 1645 explaining that there was no income from the sale of wood and timber from the estate because purchasers 'durst not come with theire carts to fetch it for feare of losinge theire horses by the soldiers . . . We durst not oppose them for feare of losinge our lives which they did threaten'. Scores of other letters from tenants tell a similar story.

It was the feeling of helpless outrage at the indiscriminate destruction and plunder which led to a remarkable protest by the ordinary people of the county against both sides in the conflict. The movement was not confined to Dorset, but had support also in Somerset and Wiltshire, as well as in Gloucestershire, but it was strongest in Dorset, particularly around Shaftesbury and the north-east of the county, an area which had been greatly affected by the passage of rival armies, and where the memory of the armed struggle against the enclosure of the royal forests during the 1620s was not dead. The Dorset Clubmen were drawn from the yeomen, husbandmen, tradesmen and others who had suffered most grievously from the war, and they took their name from the 'club' or association into which they entered for the mutual protection of their property. The leadership was provided by a few gentlemen, some younger sons of gentry families and by several of the parish clergy, in particular by Thomas Bravell, rector of Compton Abbas.

In May 1645 a great meeting of an estimated 4,000 farmers and others armed with 'clubs, swords, Bills, Pitchforks and other several weapons', was held on the open downland on Cranborne Chase near the county border with Wiltshire, and this was followed a few days later by another great meeting at Badbury Rings At these meetings a peace-keeping association was formed 'to assist one another in the mutual defence of our liberties and properties against all plunderers and all other unlawful violence'. The Clubmen of the counties of Dorset and Wiltshire adopted a Resolution declaring

> 'Wee the miserable inhabitants of the said counties being too deeply touched with the apprehension and sense of our owne past and present sufferings occasioned by these Civill and unnatural warrs . . . and foreseeing that Destruction Famine and utter Desolation will inevitably fall upon us, our wives and children ... petition for an happy peace and accommadation of the present differences, without further effusion of Christian blood.'.

In June 1645 a further meeting was held at Sturminster Newton, and a petition entitled 'The Humble Petition of the Distressed Inhabitants of the County of Dorset' demanded an end to the fighting and a peaceful settlement of the Civil War and was carried both to the King and Parliament. Apart from their wish for peace, the aims of the Clubmen are admirably summarised in the slogan which appeared on some of their banners

> 'If you offer to plunder or take our cattle,
> Be assured we will give you battle'.

During the summer of 1645 there were several minor clashes and engagements between the Clubmen and small forces of both royalist and parliamentary troops, but after the defeat of the royal army at Naseby in June 1645, it was the Parliamentary army that the Dorset Clubmen saw as the greatest threat to their lives and property. When Sir Thomas Fairfax and the parliamentary army besieged Sherborne Castle in August some of the Clubmen attempted to hinder him in any way they could. A group established themselves at Shaftesbury from where they were dispersed by parliamentary forces commanded by Oliver Cromwell; and another body of Clubmen occupied the summit of Duncliffe Hill from where they were persuaded to disperse peaceably after Cromwell had discussed their grievances with them and assured them that they would not be plundered in future.

The largest number of Clubmen, however, took up a position within the easily defended Iron Age earthwork on Hambledon Hill. On 4 August Cromwell, at the head of the parliamentary troops, found nearly 2,000 men in this stronghold, and made an unsuccessful attempt to persuade them to disperse; but the Clubmen stood firm, largely through the leadership of Thomas Bravell himself, who threatened to shoot any who gave way. For some time the Clubmen held out against the trained parliamentary troops, but they were finally overwhelmed by a cleverly-organised attack from the rear. Most of the Clubmen fled away down the steep hillside and escaped, but a dozen were killed and more than 300 were taken prisoner and locked up for the night in the nearby church of Iwerne Courtney. The next day Cromwell lectured them in the church about the error of their ways and made them promise to be well-behaved in the future. He obviously had some sympathy with their problems, and reported to Fairfax at Sherborne 'they are poor silly creatures whom if you please to let me send home they promise to be very dutiful for time to come, and will be hanged before they come out again'. The leaders were treated leniently, and even Thomas Bravell, although he was for a time deprived of the rectory of Compton Abbas, was later re-instated. The whole episode of the Clubmen did not materially affect the course of the Civil War in Dorset, but remains a rare example of concerted protest by the ordinary people of the county and highlights the hardships they had been forced to endure during the war.

Following the defeat of the royal army at Naseby, Parliamentary

The statue of Lady Mary Bankes at Kingston Lacy House.
It was Lady Bankes who in 1646 led the determined and
prolonged resistance to the Parliamentary forces during the
siege of Corfe Castle, whose key she is holding.

forces began to dominate the whole of Dorset. On 15 August 1645 Sherborne Castle was taken after a brave, but hopelessly prolonged defence by the royalist governor, Sir Lewis Dyve. In February 1646 Corfe Castle finally fell to Parliament after a long defence led by the indomitable Lady Bankes when Parliamentary soldiers managed to trick their way into the castle pretending to be reinforcements. Finally in April 1646 Portland Castle was surrendered by the royalists and Dorset was completely under the control of Parliament. The castle defences at Sherborne and Corfe were both destroyed by Parliament, with large quantities of gunpowder being used to bring down the massive walls. During 1646 and 1647 Captain Thomas Hughes was paid more than £150 for 'the demollyshinge of Corfe Castle'.

Corfe Castle under attack by Parliamentary forces in the summer of 1643. Lady Bankes and her daughters, with a handful of servants and soldiers, repulsed the final attack of this siege by throwing stones and hot embers on her attackers. The arrival of a Royalist relief force caused the Parliamentary troops to retreat – its commander, William Sydenham, leaving his supper untasted in the church and hurriedly taking a boat to Poole. Lady Bankes was then left in peace until the final siege of the castle two years later.

The triumph of Parliament was followed on 30 January 1649 by the execution of the King and the establishment of a republic. In 1650 the late King's son, Prince Charles, led a Scottish army into England in an attempt to regain the throne, only to be completely routed at Worcester by Oliver Cromwell, and were completely routed. Prince Charles fled from the battlefield and eventually reached the house of Francis Wyndham at Trent, which was then just over the border in Somerset. There the Prince was concealed for a time, before travelling on to Charmouth where he hoped to arrange for a ship from Lyme Regis to take him to France. At the last moment the plan collapsed, and he fled through Bridport and Broadwindsor, back to Trent, only narrowly escaping detection on several occasions. Finally, he left Trent again and was eventually able to get a ship from Shoreham.

During the Commonwealth Dorset was governed by a Standing Committee, consisting of prominent local gentry who had supported

The memorial near Bridport to the narrow escape of Charles II when pursued through west Dorset by Parliamentarian soldiers following his unsuccessful attempt to regain the throne at the Battle of Worcester in 1651.

the Parliamentary cause. The Committee controlled all aspects of life in the county. They confiscated and administered the estates of royalists, supervised ecclesiastical affairs, appointed ministers to parishes, cared for wounded soldiers and distributed poor relief. Constant interference in daily life did little to make the republican government popular, even among those who had been prominent critics of Charles I.

Denzil Holles had been a principal supporter of Parliament against the Crown, serving as a commander in the parliamentary army; but the failure to reach an agreement with the defeated King, his trial and brutal execution and the ever-increasing power assumed by Cromwell as Lord Protector sickened Holles. He fled into exile in Normandy, from where he wrote a long and vitriolic *Memoir* attacking Cromwell and the government over which he presided, claiming that

'The people are ruined and inslaved . . . they prostitute all to the Lust of heady violent Men. Suffer Mr Cromwell to saddle, ride, switch and spur them at his pleasures'.

Supporters of Cromwell were describing him as 'the British Hercules' and it was possibly as a counter-blast to this adulation and

The memorial in St Peter's church, Dorchester, to Denzil Holles (1599-
1680). He was the younger son of the Earl of Clare and became MP for
Dorchester. A fierce critic of Charles I, Holles became disillusioned
by Cromwell and the Commonwealth and may have been
responsible for creating the Giant on his land at Cerne Abbas
as a satire on Cromwell's claims to power.

his violent hatred of Cromwell that may have led Holles to order the
cutting of the Giant on a hillside overlooking his estate at Cerne
Abbas. This could be seen as a very public satire on Cromwell's over
weening claims to power, but no definite proof has been found, and
the Giant preserves to himself the mystery of his origin.

# RESTORATION TO REVOLUTION
## 1660-1685

The restoration of Charles II on 29 May 1660 was welcomed with great rejoicing. Most people in Dorset were glad to see the end of the Republic and a Puritan rule which had had interfered in so many aspects of daily life. The King appeared to offer religious liberty and a healing of divisions. The celebrations were particularly enthusiastic at Sherborne, the most fervently royalist of all the Dorset towns. Wine, beer and bread were freely available, processions of jubilant townspeople were led through the streets by the local gentry. Effigies of Cromwell and the regicides were burnt, and bonfires blazed around the town. Even in Puritan strongholds such as Dorchester and Lyme Regis, the church bells were rung and celebrations were held to mark the King's return.

With the restoration of Charles II came the return of the Church of England with its hierarchy of bishops, archdeacons, canons, rectors and vicars, together with all the power of the ecclesiastical courts over matters ranging from wills, marriage and religious belief to personal morality, slander and libel. Clergy who had been ejected from their parishes during the Commonwealth regained their parishes, together with their rights to tithes, glebe land and parish dues. The use of the Book of Common Prayer was revived, and the interior arrangement of parish churches was restored, with the altar at the east end of the chancel. The essential link between the monarch and the church was emphasised by the erection of the royal coat of arms, and appropriate scriptural texts urging obedience to established authority which appeared on the walls of churches, examples of which may still be seen at Cerne Abbas and Puddletown. At Dorchester the royal arms had been hidden in 1649, and in 1661 the churchwardens of All Saints' church paid £1 1s 0d for 'putting up the Kinge's Armes', and a further £3 0s 0d for gilding them. At the same time Dorchester Corporation

The Royal Arms of Charles II, in All Saints church, Dorchester.

welcomed the return of Denzil Holles and presented him with 'a gallon of sack and two gallons of French wine at his coming to Towne and a sugar loafe'.

Also restored in 1660 were the Assize Courts held twice each year in Dorchester, the government of the county by justices of the peace meeting in Quarter Sessions, and authority exercised in each parish by voluntary officials, the churchwardens and the overseers of the poor. The crucial rôle of the parish officers in village life throughout Dorset during the later seventeenth century is evident from the many surviving churchwardens' accounts, of which those from Puddletown during the 1660s and 1670s are an example. They paid for repairs and maintenance of the church, for a new Book of Common Prayer, for bread and wine for the sacrament, for washing the vicar's surplice and for sweeping the church interior, oiling the clock and the clerk who was paid for ringing the 8 o'clock curfew. They provided new bell ropes and paid the ringers each year for peals to celebrate the King's birthday, the failure of the Gunpowder Plot and also Oakapple Day [29 May] the date of the King's Restoration. They contributed to the repatriation of English sailors captured by Turkish pirates in the Mediterranean, to seamen who claimed to have been shipwrecked, to lame and wounded soldiers and to a seemingly constant stream of 'loose and idle persons' demanding poor relief, and travellers who demanded help having 'lost all by fire'.

A regular expense was the payment made to men who brought the bodies or heads of birds and animals regarded as vermin. These included many dozens of small birds, all described as 'sparrows', as well as numerous foxes, badgers, 'polecatts', hedgehogs and others. At Cerne Abbas in one year alone, 1686, the churchwardens paid for 85 dozen 'sparrows', 37 hedgehogs, 9 polecats, 9 stoats and 4 foxes. At Thorncombe an agreed scale of payments included a shilling for the heads of foxes and martens, 4d for polecats, kites, hawks, jays and 'whoops', 2d for stoats and a dozen sparrows, and 1d for crows and magpies.

Alongside the churchwardens were the overseers of the poor, generally two in number, who served for a year. They administered the parish poor rate and distributed relief to those who were unable to maintain themselves or their families. The surveyors of the highways supervised repairs to local roads. The churchwardens also had the duty of reporting any scandalous conduct so that offenders could be brought before the church court which met at Blandford. Two churchwardens were generally elected at the Easter vestry and served this onerous and unpaid office for a year. As some recompense for their many duties it is reassuring to find each year in the accounts of Puddletown a payment of 5s 0d 'for our dinners and wrighting the accounts', and similar entries in other churchwardens' accounts.

Much of the income of churchwardens had originally come from church ales and similar parish revels, but these had mostly been abolished by Puritan pressure early in the seventeenth century, and thereafter most of the money came from church rates levied upon householders. Rates were often paid grudgingly and with reluctance, and an example of the sort of problem that a churchwarden could face is found in the records of Bothenhampton, near Bridport in 1689-90. Soon after the election of Thomas Young, an illiterate carpenter, a visitation by the archdeacon revealed a leaking church roof and a defective bell. Young was ordered to arrange urgent repairs, and believing that he had the support of his fellow-parishioners, he embarked on a major programme of church restoration. Having spent more than £17, he attempted to collect church rates only to meet a concerted refusal to pay. He had also arranged for the cracked bell to

The old parish church at Bothenhampton, photographed prior to restoration in the 1970s, and where Thomas Purdue's re-cast bell was hung in 1689. The bell is still rung, but today hangs in the tiny bell-cote of the new church at the other end of the village.

be re-cast by Thomas Purdue, a well-known bell-founder from Closworth. This work cost more than £6, and when Young was unable to pay, he was sued by Purdue. Arrested for debt, he was imprisoned in Dorchester goal for five weeks where he was obliged to pay the goaler for food and drink. An appeal for help from the archdeacon's court at Blandford fell on deaf ears, and eventually Young's case was tried before the Exchequer Court which ordered the parishioners of Bothenhampton to pay the rates and Young was released. It is pleasing to record that the re-cast bell is still in the tower at Bothenhampton and bears the name of Thomas Young, the initials of the bell-founder, Thomas Purdue, and the date 1689.

The restoration of the old forms of local government and parochial control after 1660, however, give an unwarranted impression of stability. In fact, profound changes were occurring, the population of Dorset continued to increase rapidly, growing from about 84,000 in 1640 to about 90,000 by 1700. There was more unemployment and destitution, leading to many more problems for overseers of the poor in each parish and to steeply rising poor rates.

Another major change occurred through the remarkable growth of religious nonconformity. The religious freedom granted during the Commonwealth meant that Baptist, Presbyterian, Quaker and Independent congregations were established in many towns and villages, and these continued and multiplied after the restoration in 1660 in spite of persecution by the courts of both church and state. Ministers who refused to accept the return of the Church of England were ejected from their parishes. A list of ministers ejected from their parishes in Dorset compiled a few years later names 67 men. Among them was John Wesley, the vicar of Winterborne Whitechurch, grandfather of the founder of Methodism, who refused to use the Book of Common Prayer and was reported for 'diabolically railing in the pulpit' against the newly-imposed religious orders.

After 1665 it was made illegal for ministers 'who preach in unlawful assemblies' to live within five miles of the place where they had served during the Commonwealth nor within five miles of any town. As a result of the 'Five Mile Act' , many became peripatetic preachers, travelling from one congregation to another. Many in Dorset suffered greatly from the effects of the laws against dissent. Some were imprisoned, others suffered constant raids from the militia. Spies were paid to inform upon illegal worship and to report the names of ministers and congregations. For example, Christopher Lawrence, minister of Winterborne Came, was ejected from his parish in 1662. In 1665 his house was raided by the militia where they did much damage, including the destruction of his wife's medicines with which she was accustomed to treat the poor. Later Lawrence was arrested and locked up with several other ministers in Dorchester goal. There he contracted an illness from which he later died.

Nonetheless, dissenting congregations continued to meet in Dorset, often in hamlets or remote situations where they hoped to attract least attention. At Wareham, Mr Chaplyn 'a pious and conscientious clergyman' resigned rather than accept the Act of Uniformity. Philip Lamb, the assiduous minister of Bere Regis, set up a meeting house at Winterborne Kingston and attracted many of his old congregation. Many of these congregations were large. For example, 300 meeting in remote Lillington near Sherborne, 300 near Lyme Regis, 100 at Beaminster, 70 at Yetminster and 70 at Over Compton. At Ryme

Intrinseca 30 Quakers were recorded. Another list of 1676 records 1,600 dissenters in Dorset. Clearly the restored Church of England had failed to secure the support of all the people after 1660, and it was this strong under-current of dissent which was to provide the backbone of support for the Duke of Monmouth when he landed at Lyme in 1685.

In 1655 the Quaker founder, George Fox, had visited Dorset and held large meetings in Poole, Dorchester, Weymouth and Lyme Regis. In 1657 he came again and recorded in his *Journal* that 'we had glorious meetings and many were turned to the Lord'. By 1668 when Fox again undertook a preaching tour of Dorset, there were 16 Quaker meeting places in the county. The Quakers' unconventional behaviour, their disruption of church services, their refusal to pay tithes, submit to ecclesiastical authority, swear oaths or even remove their hats before the justices of the peace, meant that they were subjected to even greater persecution than other sects. In 1662 more than 200 Quakers were imprisoned in Dorset, and many underwent horrific suffering whilst in goal. In spite of persecution Quaker congregations continued to grow, and on his final visit to Dorset in 1668 Fox recorded that he had held a large meeting at Ryme Intrinseca in 'one Harris his house'. This was George Harris, whose family had lived in Ryme Intrinseca for many years. After the Act of Toleration of 1689, a permanent Quaker Meeting House was established at Ryme and a dozen other places in the county.

Another way in which Dorset was changing by the second half of the seventeenth century was in the development of industries and overseas commerce. Farming remained the mainstay of the county's economy, but the textile industry also continued to be important, and the manufacture of new cloth such as serge, and lighter fabrics was introduced, while the production of old 'kersies' or coarser fabrics continued. An inventory of the goods of John Dyett, a mercer from Bere Regis in 1662, includes dowlais, canvas, buckram, linen and calico worth more than £30. The knitting of stockings provided employment for many people, and Daniel Defoe noted at Wimborne 'the inhabitants who are many, and poor, are chiefly maintained by the manufacture of knitting stockings, which employs a great part indeed of the county of Dorset'. He also claimed that the best stockings in

Stone-quarrying on the Island of Portland. Vast quantities of the high-quality stone were extracted following Wren's decision to use it for rebuilding St Paul's Cathedral and the city churches in London after the Fire of 1666. This late-eighteenth entury view by Samuel Hieronymus Grimm illustrates the difficulty of getting large blocks from the quarries to the ships.

England were made at Stalbridge, but mentioned that the invention of a 'stocking engine' was affecting the hand knitting trade. At Poole he commented on the export of 'all sorts of wearing apparel'. Silk manufacture had been introduced at Sherborne and Cerne Abbas; pottery provided employment at Poole and on the surrounding heath, as did lace-making around Blandford Forum. Poole was also heavily involved in the Newfoundland fishery; taking goods for trade as well as bringing back fish and furs. This lucrative trade was shared by the other Dorset ports and brought great wealth to the county. The rope and sailcloth industry of Bridport, Beaminster, Broadwindsor and throughout south Somerset continued to provide much employment.

Quarrying provided an important source of wealth and employment in both production and shipping. The great period of popularity of the stone from Purbeck, the so-called 'marble' which could be polished, occurred during the Middle Ages when it was extensively used for churches and monuments, but quarrying continued and the stone was used for buildings, roofs and paving slabs, much of it exported from Swanage and Poole. A dramatic increase in demand for Portland stone occurred during the seventeenth century. Although there are isolated references to its use in the Middle Ages, this was relatively insignificant. When John Leland visited

Portland in about 1540 he was fascinated by the island, its isolation and the suspicious inhabitants, and wrote a long account of what he saw, but he does not mention the quarries. By 1635 when the Cornish traveller, Peter Mundy, visited Portland the stone was already being extensively used by Inigo Jones for repairs to the old cathedral of St Paul's in London, and on the Banqueting House in Whitehall. Mundy described the busy scene which he saw at the quarries, '. . . I went to the hewers of stone, which was carried for the reparation of St Paules church in London. There were about 200 workmen, some hewing out of the cliffe alofte, some squareinge, some carrying down, others ladeinge'. After the Fire of London in 1666 Portland stone was chosen by Sir Christopher Wren for the new St Paul's Cathedral and for many of the new churches in the city. This provided excellent publicity for the stone and created an enormous and continuing demand for it. An indication of how extensively Portland stone was used in the rebuilding of St Paul's may be gained from the Cathedral accounts which show that from the time the rebuilding could start in 1674 till Michaelmas 1700, when the Dome still had to be erected, 50,332 tons of Portland stone worth £28,065 16 7¾d had been used.

An ancient custom gave tenants of the Royal Manor of Portland the right to a half share of the 12d duty levied on every ton of stone raised from the common land and exported from the Island. The other half went to the Crown. In 1664 Charles II granted an extra 3d per ton to the Islanders in gratitude for their loyalty during the Civil War, so that they received 9d and the Crown 3d per ton. The insistence of the quarrymen on this right and their strict adherence to other ancient and complex customs which were observed on the Island exasperated Wren and there were constant disputes. In 1697 Wren himself travelled to Portland in an attempt to find some solution to the recurrent problems. The Portlanders continued to cling tenaciously to their ancient privileges, however, just as later they were able to resist all attempts to change the manorial government, agricultural practices and the lay-out of the arable fields on the Island.

Fire was a major hazard of life in the crowded, thatched-roofed towns and villages of Dorset. Besides many smaller fires, there were major conflagrations at Blandford in 1579 and 1677, Bere Regis in 1635, Beaminster in 1644 and 1684, Dorchester in 1613 and 1622,

Strip-fields near Portland Bill. The large number of small freehold tenants
on this Royal Manor meant that it was impossible to secure agreements
for enclosure, and more of the ancient field patterns survive here
than anywhere else in Dorset.

and Milton Abbas in 1658. Notwithstanding the obvious dangers,
many people were careless. At Wimborne Minster in 1629 the justices
found that Widow Gaye, who lived 'in the heart and middle of the
town', and who brewed great quantities of beer in her house, had 'a
flew or chimney made of timber to the great danger of the whole
towne'. The hooks for pulling the burning thatch from roofs can still
be seen at Bere Regis, and the buckets for water are still hung in the
church at Puddletown. In 1676 Dorchester Corporation bought a fire
engine, ladders 'and other things, fitt and necessary for quenching of
fier'.

   An unusual description of Dorset in about 1685 is provided by the
intrepid traveller, Celia Fiennes, who made journeys throughout
England at a time when such extensive sight-seeing was rare,
particularly for a single woman. Her first journey in Dorset was from
Salisbury through Cranborne Chase to Blandford which she describes
as 'a pretty neate country town'. She also visited Wareham and Poole
and was taken to Brownsea Island where she was fascinated by the
production of 'copperas' or green vitriol, used in dyeing, tanning and
ink production. It was obtained by boiling the liquor from the iron
pyrites rocks on the Island and allowing the material to crystallise.

Celia Fiennes was also impressed by the lobsters, crabs and shrimps obtainable on the Island, 'there I eate some very good'. She commented on the stone quarries on the Isle of Purbeck, on the oil-bearing shale along the cliffs around Swanage 'that are so oyly as the poor burn it for fire . . . but it has a strong offensive smell', and by the dramatic ruins of Corfe Castle which had been partially demolished only 40 years earlier. At Tyneham she mentioned the manor house 'a pretty large house but very old timber built', and again the sea-food 'there I eate the best lobsters and crabs being boiled in the sea water and scarce cold, very large and sweet'. At Dorchester Celia Fiennes commented that 'the town lookes compact . . . the Market-place is spacious, the Church very handsome and full of galleryes'. Continuing on to Bridport she found 'the wayes are stony and very narrow'. At nearby Bradpole her eye for the unusual noted that her relation, a Mr Newbery of Wooth Grange, was 'a man of many whymseys [who] would keep no woman servants, had all washing, ironing, dairy, etc all performed by men, his house looks like a little village when you come into the yard, so many little buildings . . .'. Finally, she came to Lyme Regis where she was greatly impressed by the Cobb, by the fertile countryside and by the steep narrow roads. Returning to Dorchester and thence to Blandford 'we pass over Woodbery Hill eminent for a great Faire that is kept there of all things'. She stayed with another relative, Thomas Erle of Charborough in his 'new-built house on the brow of a hill whence you have large prospects'.

Soon after the visits of Celia Fiennes, the peaceful lives of the inhabitants of the Dorset manor houses, farms and cottages which she saw were to be devastated by the events following the landing of the Duke of Monmouth at Lyme Regis on 11 June 1685, the enthusiastic welcome which supported him all the way to defeat at Sedgemoor on 6 July and the appalling retribution which ensued.

# THE MONMOUTH REBELLION AND BLOODY ASSIZE

The Monmouth Rebellion was the most remarkable popular uprising ever to occur in Dorset and the neighbouring counties. It was provoked not by poverty, hunger or economic conditions, but by a perceived threat to the Protestant religion, and to religious liberty. The gruesome punishments inflicted on Monmouth's followers left a deep mark on popular memory which has still not been entirely forgotten. Throughout the seventeenth century the one sentiment that united most of the people of England was fear and detestation of Catholicism. During the later years of the reign of Charles II, there was growing anxiety over the prospect of his Catholic brother, James, succeeding to the throne and imposing his religion upon the whole country. When Charles II died in February 1685 there were many who thought that his illegitimate son, the Protestant Duke of Monmouth, should be king. Nonetheless, James II succeeded his brother and

A nineteenth century view of the Cobb at Lyme Regis. It was on the beach in the foreground that the Duke of Monmouth began his ill-fated attempt to seize the Crown in 1685.

James, Duke of Monmouth, the illegitimate son of Charles II. His inadequate leadership of the futile rebellion against his Catholic uncle James II in 1685, brought hideous retribution and enormous suffering to his idealistic but misguided followers.

pledged to protect the law and the Church of England.

The young, handsome though ineffectual Duke had made a triumphal progress through the West Country in 1680, encouraged by the Dorset landowner and leading politician, Anthony Ashley Cooper, Earl of Shaftesbury. Monmouth was received by many of the gentry families and was welcomed by large crowds wherever he went. Three years later he was forced to flee to Holland with a small group of supporters – and it was from Holland that the abortive attempt to seize the throne from James II was launched on 11 June 1685 when Monmouth landed with 82 men at Lyme Regis.

No doubt Lyme was chosen because of its Puritan tradition and memories of its heroic resistance to the royal forces during the Civil War, and certainly Monmouth was received with great rejoicing and cheering crowds. He stayed at Lyme for a week, while recruits from east Devon, west Dorset and south Somerset flocked to join his army.

Most of these supporters were serious, upright and god-fearing men, smallholders, craftsmen and textile workers, but only a few gentry or wealthy farmers joined him. On 18 June Monmouth marched his motley, enthusiastic, but untrained army from Lyme Regis to Taunton where he received another rapturous welcome, the number of his followers swelled to nearly 4,000, and he was proclaimed king. The final annihilation of his force at Sedgemoor on the night of 5-6 July 1685 seems in retrospect to have been inevitable. His followers were quite unable to cope with a trained royal army and suffered a crushing defeat. Monmouth himself fled from the battlefield and was later captured on Horton Heath in east Dorset cowering in a ditch, disguised as a shepherd. Ten days later he was executed on Tower Hill.

After the rebellion terrible retribution swiftly followed. Many of Monmouth's supporters who had not been slaughtered at Sedgemoor were brought for trial before Assizes held at Winchester, Salisbury, Dorchester, Exeter, Taunton and Wells. At Dorchester nearly 350 men were tried in what proved to be the most dreadful of all the Assizes. Awaiting trial, the prisoners were crowded into the county goal which was soon full to overflowing, and All Saints' church was used to accommodate the rest. The conditions for them were appalling. After the Assize the church had to be fumigated, and later the churchwardens claimed £13 0s 6d 'towards the reparation of the church when made a prison for Monmouth's soldiers, itt being then demollished by them'.

The notoriously brutal Chief Justice Judge Jeffreys arrived in Dorchester from Salisbury and lodged in a fine house across the road from Shire Hall. Great pressure was put upon the prisoners to plead guilty and they were told that if they did they would receive pardons. In fact, this proved to be false, and merely meant that no witnesses were required to give evidence against them. Their guilty pleas enabled Jeffreys to impose the death penalty even more quickly than he would otherwise have done. In fact, 74 men were sentenced to death at Dorchester, and a further 175 were sentenced to transportation. The executions took place almost immediately and batches of prisoners were sent to various parts of the county to be executed from Lyme Regis to Wareham and from Weymouth to Sherborne, so that the impact and the warning of the hideous consequences of rebellion

*The Capture of the Duke of Monmouth.* A contemporary print showing the terrified Monmouth, disguised as a shepherd, discovered by the royal troops while hiding in a ditch on Horton Heath. He was executed on 15 July 1685, only ten days after the defeat of his followers at the Battle of Sedgemoor. The ash under which he was found has since been replaced by a successor, to which a plaque recording his capture is nailed.

should be as widespread as possible. In Lyme Regis 12 men were hanged, drawn and quartered near the place where Monmouth had landed. The whole business was made much worse by the gruesome practice of burning entrails, quartering the corpses and making a long-term exhibition of the dismembered parts, all designed as an awful warning. The accounts for several Dorset parishes contain references to costs occurred in the execution and display of rebels. At Wyke Regis 12s 6d was spent 'for hanging the Rebels' quarters', including 2s od for beer for the men who undertook the task. The Weymouth accounts include the following entry:

'14th October 1685
To a bill of disbursements for ye gallows,
Burning and Boyling ye Rebels executed by
Order att this Towne     £16-4-8'

Lord Chief Justice George Jeffreys, whose summary
verdicts on the Monmouth rebels, and the dreadful punishments
immediately inflicted upon them, ensured that his name
remained reviled and hated throughout the West Country.

Large numbers of rebels were transported to the West Indies where
they were sold to plantation-owners, becoming indentured servants
for ten years. During the autumn of 1685 several shiploads left
Weymouth, including 91 on the inappropriately-named *Happy
Return*. Among those who were transported was Azariah Pinney, one
of the few wealthy persons of good family who had joined
Monmouth. He was a member of a long-established west Dorset
family, his father, John Pinney, had been the minister for
Broadwindsor during the Commonwealth. The family possessed land
in Bettiscombe, and had a considerable lace-making and textile
business. When Azariah was sentenced at Dorchester for his part in
the Monmouth affair, his family was able to use its wealth and
influence to secure better treatment for him, and he was transported
as a free emigrant. His sister, Hester, used her entire savings of £65 as
a ransom for her brother, while Azariah's elder brother, Nathaniel,
spent more than £100 on equipping him for the journey to the West
Indies on the *Rose*. Thanks to the money paid by his relatives, once in
the West Indies he was free to act as agent for other members of the
family, selling lace and a variety of other goods, and building up a

V ♦

*Severall of y̓ Rebells hang'd upon a Tree*

The 5 of Diamonds, from a set of contemporary playing cards issued after the Rebellion. Portrayals such as this of the suffering of the rebels did much to increase the horror felt at the treatment endured by simple men, concerned only to protect the Protestant religion.

substantial business. Eventually, he became a plantation-owner and established a secure fortune; in 1696 he became a member of the House of Assembly and later was Treasurer of the islands. Like so many others, a few days under Monmouth's standard dramatically changed Azariah Pinney's whole life, though few of his fellow rebels derived similar profit from their involvement in the rising.

\* \* \*

The Stuart period lasted until the death of Queen Anne in 1713, but the story of the overthrow of James II in 1688 by William of Orange, the so-called 'Glorious Revolution' which followed, circumscribing the power of the monarchy, and England's long involvement in foreign conflict, culminating in the European victories of the Duke of Marlborough, needs to be considered in the context of the eighteenth century. A description of Dorset at the beginning of the eighteenth century provides both a convenient conclusion and a good comparison with the situation two centuries earlier when Henry VII inaugurated the Tudor dynasty.

The description is contained in Daniel Defoe's *Tour through England and Wales*. Daniel Defoe (1660-1731) is probably best known as the author of novels such as *Robinson Crusoe*, and he wrote his *Tour* with the express purpose of earning money from its publication. Happily, it also provides the most graphic contemporary account of the state of the country prior to the vast changes which were to be caused by an increase in population and industrialisation.

In crossing the open downland between Salisbury and Shaftesbury Defoe encountered a common problem for travellers. With no signposts and 'neither house nor town in view' it was not easy to keep to the correct road, except that everywhere on the downs directions could be obtained from 'shepherds feeding or keeping their vast flocks of sheep'. From Shaftesbury, then in decline and 'now a sorry town', Defoe looked across the Blackmore Vale 'rich, fertile and populous'. At several places during his journey he had lamented the decline in local markets in the face of private deals struck in inns and private houses. Thus he found Shaftesbury, which had previously been such a busy market town, in decline and described it as 'now a sorry town'. At Wimborne he saw 'nothing remarkable but the church which is indeed a very great one'. He was impressed by the situation of Poole and by the prosperous Newfoundland fishery . Wareham he thought 'a neat town and full of people', whilst on the Isle of Purbeck he saw the 'vast quarreys of stone' which supplied London with paving slabs. Crossing Morden Heath he visited the duck decoy and observed a large eagle caught in a trap set to protect the decoy ducks from predators. Weymouth he considered to be 'a sweet clean, agreeable town', its ships trading with France, Portugal, Spain, Virginia and Newfoundland. On the Island of Portland he watched admiringly as large blocks of stone were cut out at one of the quarrys to be dispatched to London. He also noted the twin castles at Sandsfoot and Portland, and two lighthouses which had recently been set up to warn ships of the dangers of the strong currents of the Portland Race off the coast. Continuing his journey westward, Defoe was impressed by the swannery and duck decoy at Abbotsbury where he claimed to have seen at least 8,000 swans. Abbotsbury itself he described as 'a town anciently famous for a great monastery, and now eminent for nothing but its ruins'.

At Bridport he saw many boats fishing for mackerel, but apparently saw little remarkable in the town itself. Coming to Lyme Regis, Defoe remarked that it was 'made famous by the landing of the Duke of Monmouth and his unfortunate troop'. Again, he was impressed by the busy port, by the Cobb and by the number of ships trading all over Europe. Above all, however, he observed the good relations between all classes of the community at Lyme, and concluded the inhabitants to be 'some of the most polite and well bred people in the isle of Britain'.

Travelling inland, Defoe commented on the bonelace industry of Blandford 'the finest bonelace in England' which, he claimed, could be sold at £30 per yard. At Stalbridge he found the town and the surrounding countryside occupied in knitting stockings.

Finally, Defoe's visit to Dorchester resulted in an eulogy on the town and the religious tolerance which he observed there. As a dissenter, Defoe had himself suffered religious persecution, and it was with evident personal feeling that he wrote the following description of Dorchester. His praise of the town makes an agreeable conclusion to this account of Dorset under the Tudors and Stuarts.

'From hence we turn'd up to Dorchester, the county town, tho' not the largest town in the county; Dorchester is indeed a pleasant agreeable town to live in, and where I thought the people seem'd less divided into factions and parties, than in other places; for though here are divisions and the people are not all of one mind, either as to religion, or politicks, yet they did not seem to separate with so much animosity as in other places . . . The town is populous, tho' not large, the streets broad, but the buildings old, and low; however, there is good company and a good deal of it; and a man that coveted a retreat in this world might as agreeably spend his time, and as well in Dorchester, as in any town I know in England'.

# FURTHER READING

The volumes of the *Proceedings* of the Dorset Natural History & Archaeological Society and those of Somerset and Dorset *Notes & Queries* provide a vast amount of information on the archaeology and history of Dorset. Together with the magisterial *History of Dorset* by John Hutchins, first published in two volumes in 1774, enlarged into four volumes in 1861-70, they provide the starting point for any historical research in the county. In addition, the volumes of the *Royal Commission on Historical Monuments* supply a comprehensive coverage of the architecture and archaeology of Dorset. The following are some more specific works on Tudor and Stuart Dorset:

Bayley, A.R., *The Civil War in Dorset*, 1910
Bettey, J.H., *Rural Life in Wessex*, 1977
Bettey J.H., *The Casebook of Sir Francis Ashley 1614-35*, (Dorset Record Society), 1981
Bettey J.H., *Wessex from AD1000*, 1986
Bettey J.H., *The Suppression of the Monasteries in the West Country*, 1989
Earle P., *Monmouth's Rebels*, 1987
Hearing T., *Dorset Quarter Sessions Order Book 1625-38*, 2006
Lloyd R., *Dorset Elizabethans*, 1967
Oswald A., *Country Houses of Dorset*, (2nd Edn.) 1959
Pares R., *A West Indian Fortune*, 1950
Taylor C., *The Making of the English Landscape: Dorset*, 1970
Underdown D., *Revel, Riot and Rebellion*, 1985
Underdown D., *Fire from Heaven*, 1992
Wigfield W.M., *The Monmouth Rebellion*, 1980

# ACKNOWLEDGEMENTS

The help received in the preparation of this book is gratefully acknowledged. David Burnett has carefully edited the text and has provided most of the illustrations. Jo Draper has always been willing to share her knowledge of Dorset history and I am indebted to Hugh Jacques and all the archivists at the Dorset Record Office and to Steven Hobbs and his colleagues at the Salisbury Diocesan Record Office in Trowbridge. The collections at Dorset County Museum and Dorset County Library have been invaluable in my research. My former colleagues at the University of Bristol, Mick Aston and Robert Machin have provided help and suggestions. Christopher Taylor's work on the development of the Dorset landscape has been a constant source of inspiration.

I am grateful to Christopher Chaplin for the map on page 6 and to the following for allowing the inclusion of illustrations in their possession or for which they hold the copyright: His Grace the Duke of Buccleuch and Queensbury; 77: British Library; 81: © Crown Copyright.NMR; 3, 4, 10, 16, 31 (both), 32 (left), 53 (bottom), 62, 65, 67, 69: Dorset County Museum; 24, 76: Dovecote Press Collection; 7, 8, 9, 10, 12, 13, 21, 22, 27, 30 (both), 32, 35, 37, 39, 41 (both), 45, 50, 52, 53 (top), 57, 63, 64, 72, 74, 79, 80, back cover: English Heritage.NMR; 17, 40, 51: National Portrait Gallery (London); 38, 53.

The illustration on the front cover is a detail from *Corfe Castle in the Beauteous Isle of Purbeck* by Isabel Saul (1895-c1982), with thanks to the Russell-Cotes Museum and Art Gallery, Bournemouth, UK, and the Bridgeman Art Library. The painting was exhibited in 1940, but sadly little is known about Isabel Saul beyond the fact that she was born and lived in Southbourne. After attending Bournemouth Municipal School of Art she went on to work in watercolours and tempera, specialising in ecclesiastical subjects and portraits. The Dovecote Press would welcome any further information about Isabel Saul.

# INDEX

*The*

# DISCOVER DORSET

*Series of Books*

A series of paperback books providing informative illustrated
introductions to Dorset's history, culture and way of life.
The following titles have so far been published.

BLACKMORE VALE *Hilary Townsend*

BRIDGES *David McFetrich and Jo Parsons*

CASTLES & FORTS *Colin Pomeroy*   COAST & SEA *Sarah Welton*

CRANBORNE CHASE *Desmond Hawkins*

DOWNS, MEADOWS & PASTURES *Jim White*

DRESS & TEXTILES *Rachel Worth*

FARMHOUSES & COTTAGES *Michael Billett*

FARMING *J.H.Bettey*   FOLLIES *Jonathan Holt*

FOSSILS *Richard Edmonds*   GEOLOGY *Paul Ensom*

THE GEORGIANS *Jo Draper*   HEATHLANDS *Lesley Haskins*

THE INDUSTRIAL PAST *Peter Stanier*

ISLE OF PURBECK *Paul Hyland*   LEGENDS *Jeremy Harte*

LOST VILLAGES *Linda Viner*   MILLS *Peter Stanier*

PORTLAND *Stuart Morris*   POTTERY *Penny Copland-Griffiths*

THE PREHISTORIC AGE *Bill Putnam*

RAILWAY STATIONS *Mike Oakley*

REGENCY, RIOT & REFORM *Jo Draper*

RIVERS & STREAMS *John Wright*   THE ROMANS *Bill Putnam*

SAXONS & VIKINGS *David Hinton*   SHIPWRECKS *Maureen Attwooll*

STONE QUARRYING *Jo Thomas*   TUDORS & STUARTS *J.H. Bettey*

THE VICTORIANS *Jude James*   WOODLANDS *Anne Horsfall*

All the books about Dorset published by The Dovecote Press
are available in bookshops throughout the county,
or in case of difficulty direct from the publishers.
The Dovecote Press Ltd, Stanbridge,
Wimborne Minster, Dorset BH21 4JD
Tel: 01258 840549   www.dovecotepress.com